T0243542

Praise for
Busy Is A Four-Letter Word

In Kishshana Palmer's captivating book *Busy Is A Four-Letter Word*, I found myself immersed in a world of tangible tools and invaluable insights that have transformed the way I will approach my leadership as a Black woman CEO from now on. Kishshana's writing is not only relatable and witty, but also backed by thorough research, making it an indispensable resource for anyone looking to navigate the challenges of a demanding career while maintaining their sanity.

What sets this book apart is Kishshana's unique approach of relating leadership tips to scenes from two iconic sitcoms from the 80s – *A Different World* and *The Golden Girls*. By drawing parallels between these beloved shows and real-life leadership scenarios, Kishshana injects a sense of familiarity and humor into her advice, making it all the more accessible and relevant.

But what truly sets *Busy Is A Four-Letter Word* apart is Kishshana's genius and humanity that shine through every page. It feels as though she is lovingly coaching and pushing leaders to be their best whole-hearted selves, making the journey to success not only manageable but also deeply fulfilling.

Reading this book felt like receiving the best hug I never knew I needed – comforting, reassuring, and empowering all at once. I cannot recommend it highly enough to every leader and leader-in-training out there. Kishshana Palmer's *Busy Is A Four-Letter Word* is a must-read that will undoubtedly leave a lasting impact on your leadership journey.

—Dr. Angela Glymph
CEO of Peer Health Exchange

The first time I saw Kishshana speaking on a stage I was instantaneously impressed by her style, specifically her stiletto shoes. It didn't take much longer for me to be inspired by her wisdom and wit. A burned-out vice president at a national nonprofit at the time, I credit Kishshana with saving me from prematurely ending my career. Her coaching and example as an entrepreneur and mom have helped me navigate my own life redesign and career pivot. *Busy Is A Four-Letter Word* will help you recognize the systems, practices, and beliefs that keep you running ragged and provides practical guidance to live a more balanced life on purpose and your own terms. It's a ticket to freedom!

—Maria Dautruche
Founder, dopwell group LLC

BUSY
IS A
FOUR-LETTER
WORD

A GUIDE TO ACHIEVING
MORE BY DOING **LESS**

BUSY
IS A
FOUR-LETTER
WORD

KISHSHANA PALMER

WILEY

Published by John Wiley & Sons, Inc., Hoboken, New Jersey.
Published simultaneously in Canada.

For general information on our other products and services or for technical support, please contact our Customer Care Department within the United States at (800) 762-2974, outside the United States at (317) 572-3993 or fax (317) 572-4002.

Wiley also publishes its books in a variety of electronic formats. Some content that appears in print may not be available in electronic formats. For more information about Wiley products, visit our web site at www.wiley.com.

Library of Congress Cataloging-in-Publication Data Is Available:

ISBN 9781394243198 (Cloth)
ISBN 9781394243204 (ePub)
ISBN 9781394243211 (ePDF)
ISBN 9781394308453 (oBook)

Cover Design and Image: © Alicia L. Fitch
Author Photo: Courtesy of Mary Claire Stewart

SKY10092526_120324

Contents

Foreword

Dr. Robert S. Harvey

To be busy, or not to be busy: *that is the question.*

For decades, our lives have become progressively faster. What was at one time a necessary symptom reserved for outlier professionals—physicians, politicians, and preachers [because alliteration is queen]—has now rotted the whole. Rot, though a strong word choice you might argue, is apropos because *missing time with family, juggling back-to-back calendar items, forgetting to eat, operating off caffeine, and sleeping less than elephant seals* is for so many, a brag. Imagine that: bragging about the dethreading of one's relationships, the destruction of one's body, and in so many ways, the dissipation of one's soul.

Again, strong word choices, I know.

My maternal grandmother, Alma ['Granny'], was a Black woman born during the *Progressive Era* where social activism and political reform swept the nation. She lived the first two decades of her life in Shannon, Mississippi, named after Samuel Shannon, who purchased land at that location from Chickasaw Chief Itawamba in the early 1800s. For a century, it was known for a creek, a church, corn, and cotton gin. To this very day, the town website prides itself on being "the quiet side of the country." Our family maintains acres of land in that town where my visits affirm that flowing creeks and a slowed-paced for doing *just about everything* continue to make Shannon what it is. As she once said, "We didn't have much, but we had it all."

In the 1940s, granny boarded a northbound train for St. Louis, a crowded, fast, *and busy* city of more than 800,000 residents trying to make sense of itself, its economy, and its culture during World War II. Within a matter of months, what was at once a slow life, marked by its reputation for simplicity and stillness, became a life consumed by "conspicuous consumption," a concept coined by economist Thorstein Veblen. Buicks, Cadillacs, furs, costume jewelry, and expanding closets for more clothes than we'd ever wear. *More stuff, less time* became the new reputational mark of superiority. The answer in this new city, with new opportunities and new industries and new homes and new money was: *to be busy*. Lest you judge me as a judge of my granny, she was not an anomaly, but the norm. She was part of the turning tide in this nation where compounding capitalism and growing militarism demanded more of life than a creek, a church, corn, and cotton gin. Marked by racism and classism and sexism, she fueled her success as an emerging mother of four as most did: *busyness*. Did she miss the stillness? Did she long for simplicity? Did she ever want the sounds of the creek passing through the town? I will never know. But what I do know is that America has always had a way of marking our relationships, our bodies, and our souls with a branding that transcends our choice—and the brand we've been forced to endure since the 40s is: *to be busy*.

A couple of years ago, I started color-coding my calendar as a way of signaling to my brain the distinction between *internal meetings, external meetings, travel, focused work blocks (affectionately titled, 'do not schedule'), and deliverables*. In effect, I started color-coding my busyness. Because, if I must be busy, it should at least have coordinated color-codes and stylistic labeling. Right? This year, I discovered that one of the underlying causes of the *busyness-for-busyness-sake-syndrome* ('BS') is at worst: rationalism. Think for a moment on the people who've seemed to take "busy" and tossed it out the window. You know. . .your drunk uncle at the holiday barbecue, or the loquacious neighbor who's retired and sits on the front porch watching people because what else do they have to do? It was in fact, Gottfried Leibniz, the German philosopher who contented: "The senses, although they are necessary for all our actual knowledge, are not sufficient to give us the whole of it, since the senses never give anything but instances. . ."[1] Imagine ignoring that *sense*

---

[1] Gottfried Wilhelm Leibniz, 1704, New Essays on Human Understanding, Preface, pp. 150

of what you feel deep within your body and your soul. Imagine disregarding the fullness of the sense you are experiencing within your relationships that *something must give.* That sense of a new way and a new normal needing to emerge, only for you to rationalize yourself to busyness.

At its worst—*our calendar coding and half-day work blocks and back-to-back meetings and phone notifications from Slack and Asana and Teams and Trello, and the push feature, walking pads underneath our desks versus taking a break to go for a walk, passive usage of 'just text me if you need anything' while on vacation, or sneaking a peek at our missed messages while at the basketball game or watching dance practice*—are the signs, symptoms, and sins of our rationalization.

Now, in this productivity era (forever revolutionized by a global pandemic) where we are always attached to our productivity, I propose that we can trust our senses again. What might it look like to rediscover, or for many of *us* (yes, us: because who I am to not be consumed by the smog of 'BS': *busyness-for-busyness-sake-syndrome?*), discover for the first time what it means to live and lean into the *quiet side of ourselves.* Quiet, not to be confused with nothingness or lacking productivity or neglecting one's pursuit of meaningfulness. But instead, a quietness that privileges the instinctual beauty of what our senses compel of us: to deepen our relationships through quality time and intimacy, to center ourselves within the peculiarly beautiful moments that come-and-go fleetingly like the seconds of a baby's belly laugh, or to tend to our souls and heart that we might see one another more fully.

We often are intrigued by the routines and schedules of those who are the most successful—what time they wake up, how much they get done in a day, their workout regimen, or how many books they read in a year. And we assume, falsely, that those are the trappings (literally, traps) of how they've *made it* to success. In *Busy is a*

Four-Letter Word, Kishshana offers an alternative thesis: what if the patterns that shape our successes and triumphs and conquering's are formed and informed by how busy-less we are? What if it is only by asking what we can give up, what stuff we can surrender, what northbound trains we can miss that permits us to unravel the logic of success in this world? This is a book about counter-logic, counter-rationalism, and counterculture. Through anecdotes that nudge at the human condition, and through television icons that mirror the complexity of our ordinariness, and through laughter that pierces the seriousness we often veil ourselves with, Kishshana invites us to reconsider what we hold true about ourselves individually, communally, and organizationally.

Nagging at many of you who have picked-up this book is a simple question: *how can I lead a deeply meaningful and robustly successful life by doing less?* The answer, too, is simple: by being at peace within oneself and with one's senses.

In that peace, you might not have much, but you'll have it all.

THANK YOU FOR BEING A FRIEND

"I'm so busy, I've had this headache for three years!"
— Jean, *The Golden Girls*

Picture it: Miami, 1985. Four fabulous ladies were living together and taking on the world, one cheesecake at a time. Of course, I'm talking about the one and only *The Golden Girls*. As a kid watching that show, I never imagined the profound life lessons it would impart to me. I was a "busy" kid. As a Gen Xer I was also a latch-key kid so I *found* things to do with my time. My days were full of school, the library, books, and church! In middle school, I was class president, morning announcer, and lead singer in the chorus. And at church, I was in the choir, in Pathfinders Club (shout out to all my fellow 7th Day Kids), on the drill team, and in drum core … jusssst to name a few. I would stay up for hours into the middle of the night reading books. I'm not gonna lie. I loved all the inappropriate stuff for my age like Harlequin romance and Danielle Steele novels right alongside the Babysitters Club and the Hardy Boys. My fourth-grade teacher, Mrs. Spradley, told my parents that these types of books were "advanced." She should *not* have said that! All my dad heard was "advanced" and said, "Well, at least she's reading! My parents were just happy I was keeping myself busy. I wanted to be a grown-up so bad! They always looked like they had something important to do and somewhere to be. So I wanted IN (queue my first job at 14)!

I didn't know why then (even though I know now) but one episode that has really stuck with me over the years is when, in *The Golden Girls*, Dorothy's friend Jean visits. Jean laments, "I'm so busy, I've had this headache for three years!" To which the ever-wise Sophia retorts, "*Busy* is a four-letter word for idiots!" Shoot! Maybe I am just speaking for myself.

As a multi-hyphenate entrepreneur, I would stay up for hours tip-tapping at my keyboard. I used to subscribe to the "sleep is for suckas" motto. I want you to know that the only sucka there was …

Preface: Thank You for Being a Friend

ME!! It left me tired, caffeine addicted, bedraggled, anxiety driven, and eating and shopping my feelings away. My body was crying out so badly that I developed sciatica, but I had a goal to be successful. My challenge was that I didn't *know* what success meant ... to ME!

This relentless pursuit of busyness masquerading as success is actually making us sick – physically, mentally, emotionally, financially, and relationally. It's leaving us drained, dragging, anxious, and disconnected from what really matters in life.

In the pages ahead, I share insights from my own journey as a professional high achiever, entrepreneur, first-gen career woman, solo mom, and human being who got caught up in the toxic cycle of busyness. You'll learn my strategies for slowing down, streamlining your life, and prioritizing your health over a packed schedule. To be clear, I don't have it *all* figured out and I wouldn't trust anyone who says they do.

This book almost didn't get written because I was too ... busy. I hemmed and hawed about what to share, how to share it, and what would happen IF I really shared my journey to doing less so that I had a shot at achieving more. I was sure that I'd never find the time. With work travel, moving my life from the East Coast to the South, getting my "queenager" off to college, picking up the pieces of my business that nearly went bankrupt because of institutional clients with a lack of integrity who preyed on small businesses and whose leadership had no regard for paying their bills on time or keeping their word (and I am being kind and generous here because if I ever see these so-called leaders in the street ... baaaaaybeeee) alongside what seemed like a never-ending trip of WTF is going on here, I tip-tapped on this keyboard. If you read that and thought HOLY SMOKES, you have a lot going on, then, yeah ... me, too. My reality: I was afraid that you wouldn't think I knew my stuff (oooh, that's one I will get to in later chapters).

My mom often makes the joke that I came into this world running and ready to go from Day 1. I was busy! I learned to walk early, speak early, and was reading by three years old. I was selected for the gifted and talented program in second grade where the message that being "smart" was a thing to be celebrated was reinforced. And yet, at every parent-teacher conference, teachers would tell my parents that I was a "busybody" so much so that my mom told my middle school social studies teacher not to call her during her workday anymore because if I wasn't disrupting the class (I wasn't) then what was the problem? By high school, I was running EVERY DARN THING! With a job! And I studied abroad in Budapest, Hungary. And started my own choir. Dang y'all, I was building a foundation of B-U-S-Y. It all looked great on paper and helped me secure a scholarship to college. Buuuuuut! Let's put the cookie jar where we all can get to them. To my untrained 17-year-old eye, the badge of "busy" is often worn with honor. Yet, this relentless pursuit of busyness not only exhausts us but paradoxically hinders our ability to achieve true productivity and satisfaction. But I wouldn't learn that until years later.

Drawing from more than two decades of experience as a C-suite executive and consultant, I've witnessed firsthand the detrimental effects of our culture's obsession with busyness. This book is born from a blend of personal insights, professional engagements, and a heartfelt desire to shift the paradigm from being busy to being impactful.

Maybe you're like Darlene, a senior executive juggling multiple roles both at work and home. Despite her accomplishments, she felt perpetually drained and unfulfilled.

Or maybe you're more like James, an entrepreneur whose start-up's rapid growth was both his dream and his nightmare due to his unsustainable workload. Even these small bits from their stories echo a common theme in today's work culture, and they are not isolated incidents but rather reflections of a widespread challenge that demands attention and action.

These everyday leaders' stories propelled me to write this book. My goal is to guide you – the overwhelmed professional, leader, caregiver, community advocate, entrepreneur, or student – toward a path where success is not measured by how full your schedule is, but by how meaningful your actions are. Through the pages of this book, you will discover innovative strategies and practical tools that will empower you to declutter your commitments, focus on what truly matters, and reclaim your time and energy.

The Golden Girls and *A Different World* Make an Appearance!

I love a good sitcom. I'll even binge watch a juicy reality series (hello *Married at First Site* and *Love Is Blind*). But my classics still have lessons that ring true today. In this book, you'll encounter numerous references to two beloved shows of mine – *The Golden Girls* and *A Different World*. As I reflect on why I chose these as touchstones for this book, I'm struck by how perfectly these shows embody the journey from youthful ambition to seasoned wisdom. *The Golden Girls* gives us a quartet of vibrant women in their well-seasoned years, each with a lifetime of experiences behind them. They've weathered life's storms, learned hard lessons, and come out the other side with a clearer understanding of what truly matters. Their witty banter and cheesecake-fueled problem-solving sessions remind us that sometimes, slowing down and connecting with friends is the most productive thing we can do.

On the flip side, *A Different World* captures the energy and idealism of youth. Set on a college campus, it showcases young adults taking risks, chasing dreams, and often stumbling as they try to figure out who they are and what they want from life. The contrast between these two shows mirrors our own journey from the frenetic pace of our early careers to the more measured approach that is *supposed* to come with experience.

Throughout this book, you'll find me returning to characters from both shows as I explore different aspects of doing less to achieve more. Whether it's Sophia's no-nonsense wisdom, Whitley's journey from entitled princess to self-aware professional, or Dwayne's evolution from awkward nerd to confident achiever, these characters offer valuable lessons on prioritizing what's truly important on the road to success. I draw parallels between their fictional experiences and real-world for streamlining your life and focusing on what matters most. So don't be surprised if you find yourself nodding along as I reference Dorothy's dry wit or Freddie's passionate activism – these characters aren't just entertainment; they're guides on our journey to a more balanced, fulfilling life. And just like how these shows tackled serious issues with humor and heart, I approach challenges with a mix of laughter and deep reflection. After all, as Rose Nylund would say, "The older you get, the better you get. Unless you're a banana."

Before diving in, let me ask you something. Do you have a to-do list? Whether it's on paper, your computer, or your phone, how do you feel when you jot down so many tasks that you're scribbling in the margins or on the back, and you still have more to add? And how about when the day ends and you've only crossed off a couple of things? If you're anything like me, that sense of defeat and overwhelm creeps in faster than piping hot donuts coming off the conveyer belt at Krispy Kreme when the "HOT" light is on. Even if you've somehow managed to tick off 1,347 items from your list, you still feel like a failure. Because at the end of the day, what good is checking things off your to-do list if you're too burned out to enjoy your accomplishments? As Rose so wisely stated, "It's like life is a giant weenie roast, and I'm the biggest weenie!" Let's stop being weenies, shall we?

The Golden Girls

The Golden Girls is a beloved television sitcom that aired from 1985 to 1992, focusing on the lives of four older women sharing a home in Miami, Florida. The show blends humor, friendship, and social commentary, tackling issues relevant to older women with wit and warmth. The series revolves around four vibrant, single women in their golden years who become unlikely roommates. Blanche Devereaux, a Southern belle and the owner of the house, opens her home to fellow widow Rose Nylund and divorcée Dorothy Zbornak after they respond to an ad on a grocery store bulletin board. In the pilot episode, they are joined by Dorothy's 80-year-old mother, Sophia Petrillo, after her retirement home burns down.

Dorothy Zbornak (Bea Arthur):

A sharp-witted, sarcastic substitute teacher from Brooklyn, New York
Known for her deadpan humor and cutting remarks
Often the voice of reason among the group
Struggles with her self-esteem due to her failed marriage

Rose Nylund (Betty White):

A sweet, naive woman from the fictional town of St. Olaf, Minnesota
Known for her quirky stories and often misunderstood comments
Possesses hidden talents, including psychology knowledge and piano skills
Happily widowed and maintains a positive, sometimes childlike outlook on life

Blanche Devereaux (Rue McClanahan):

A flirtatious Southern belle and owner of the house
Known for her man-hungry ways and vivacious personality
Proud of her looks and charm, often exaggerating her age
Struggles with aging and self-worth issues

Preface: Thank You for Being a Friend

Sophia Petrillo (Estelle Getty):

Dorothy's feisty Sicilian mother with a sharp tongue

Known for her "Picture this ..." stories and brutally honest comments

Provides comic relief and unexpected wisdom

Originally planned as an occasional guest star but became a regular due to her popularity

A Different World

A Different World is a spin-off from *The Cosby Show* that aired from 1987 to 1993. It originally centered on Denise Huxtable (Lisa Bonet) and the life of students at Hillman College, a fictional historically Black college in Virginia. The show evolved to focus more broadly on the experiences of a diverse group of students navigating college life. It tackled significant social issues such as institutionalized racism, HIV/AIDS, and sexual assault, making it a groundbreaking series for its time.

Denise Huxtable (Lisa Bonet):

The original protagonist, daughter of Dr. Huxtable from *The Cosby Show*

Struggles to find her place and identity at Hillman College

Known for her free-spirited and somewhat naive nature

Whitley Gilbert (Jasmine Guy):

A Southern belle with a wealthy background

Known for her snobbish and materialistic demeanor

Evolves into a more compassionate and grounded character over the series

Dwayne Wayne (Kadeem Hardison):

A nerdy, intelligent student and future engineer with distinctive flip-up glasses

Known for his crush on Denise and, later, his relationship with Whitley

Grows into a confident and successful individual

Freddie Brooks (Cree Summer):

A free-spirited, socially conscious student

Known for her activism and unique fashion sense

Often provides a countercultural perspective on issues

Jaleesa Vinson (Dawnn Lewis):

A mature, responsible student who returns to college after a failed marriage

Known for her no-nonsense attitude and strong work ethic

Acts as a mentor and big sister figure to the younger students

Ron Johnson (Darryl M. Bell):

Dwayne's best friend and roommate

Known for his entrepreneurial spirit and love of partying

Struggles with balancing his ambitions and personal life

Kimberly Reese (Charnele Brown):

A premed student with a strong sense of duty and responsibility

Known for her serious and focused demeanor

Faces the pressures of academic and personal challenges

Impact and Legacy

The Golden Girls and *A Different World* have left indelible marks on television history. *The Golden Girls* broke new ground by portraying independent mature women and discussing important issues like race, class, and sexual identity. It remains a beloved classic, praised for its humor and heart. *A Different World* offered a realistic and nuanced portrayal of Black college life, addressing social issues that were often ignored by mainstream media. It provided representation and inspiration for many viewers, showing that college was not only attainable but also a place for growth and self-discovery. Both sitcoms give voice to voices normally silenced by the status quo. The field of leadership is dominated by the status quo. I learned the rules, realized they didn't really work for me, and decided to turn the mic up on everyday leaders who want to achieve more and are exhausted by having to always do more.

As you embark on this journey to reclaim your life from the clutches of busyness, you can take a page from these iconic shows. They remind us that life is not about how much we do but about the quality of our experiences and the relationships we build along the way. So, let's slow down, savor the moments, and find joy in the simple things – just like these beloved TV characters did. After all, life is too short to be anything but meaningful.

Grab a slice of cheesecake, thank your friend (that's MEEEEE) for being a friend, and let's get started on reclaiming our health and sanity from the busyness trap. After all, as Blanche would say, "I've been having a good time, and there wasn't even a man in the room!"

Bloop!!!

CHAPTER 1

THE PURSUIT OF
HAPPYLESS:
BUSY IS A FOUR-LETTER WORD

"I try to take one day at a time, but sometimes
several days attack me at once."

JENNIFER YANE

Picture it: an early Monday morning, the smell of coffee brewing, and the faint sound of *The Golden Girls* theme song playing in the background. Yes, "thank you for being a friend," indeed. My name is Kishshana Palmer, and just like the fabulous ladies of that beloved show believed, I'm here to tell you that being busy is not all it's cracked up to be.

For years, I prided myself on being the multitasking queen, juggling numerous tasks like Blanche Devereaux juggling her suitors. One of my best friends, AJ, would often tease me about my ability to talk on the phone while cooking, while putting away all the dishes and tidying up without missing a beat. But, spoiler alert, it turns out that multitasking is as effective as Rose Nylund trying to explain St. Olaf customs – it sounds impressive but often ends up being a hot mess. Oooh, I love *The Golden Girls*!

The Myth of Multitasking

Let me take you back to the days when I believed that having a packed schedule was synonymous with success. Most days, after moving swiftly through morning devotion, I would shower, get dressed, and get the kiddo ready for a.m. drop-off. I'd race for the train, often with seconds to spare before the door closes, headed to the office. Once there, I began my daily cupid shuffle of responding to emails, often while on a conference call, and simultaneously planning my to-do list for the day. I thought I was getting so much done, but in reality, I was spreading myself thinner than Sophia Petrillo's patience when dealing with Rose's stories.

It took me a really long time to accept that multitasking was a myth, a lie we tell ourselves to feel productive. Studies have shown that multitasking actually dilutes our focus, reduces productivity, and increases stress. I felt like I was losing brain cells with every open tab on my laptop. It was like trying to have a meaningful conversation while Sophia interjects with a "Picture it, Sicily ..." anecdote every few seconds. Distracting, right?

Research on Multitasking

Research by cognitive psychologists has consistently debunked the effectiveness of multitasking. One study conducted at Stanford University[1] found that heavy multitaskers were less effective at filtering out irrelevant information and took longer to switch between tasks. In other words, multitasking turns your brain into the organizational equivalent of travelers grounded at the airport trying to get the one available flight home. Chaos.

A study by the American Psychological Association found that multitasking can reduce productivity by up to 40%.[2] When we switch tasks, it takes time for our brains to adjust and refocus, leading to lost time and increased chances of making mistakes. It's like trying to read a map, text, and drive. We all think we can do it, but the number of texting while driving accidents say otherwise.

When we multitask, our brains are not doing multiple things at once. Instead, they are rapidly switching from one task to another. And, yikes, the mistakes we make are like pebbles in a jar. On their own they might be light and of little consequence but when you pick up a jar full its weighty. This constant switching not only exhausts our mental energy but also makes us more prone to errors. I realized that when I am working on too many things at once my body starts to protest. No wonder I constantly had a headache and could not understand why. My switches were burnt out. Just me? Nope.

---

[1] Wagner, Anthony. (2018). A decade of data reveals that heavy multitaskers have reduced memory. *Stanford Report*. October 25th.
[2] Clarke, Jodi. (2023). *How constantly staying busy affects our well-being*. Verywell Mind. https://www.verywellmind.com/about-us-5184564

Friend, our wires are shorted. And worse, our brains have pulled the emergency break screeching to a halt at survival mode.

The Psychological Toll of Multitasking

The toll of multitasking goes beyond just reduced productivity. It also affects our mental health. Chronic multitasking can lead to increased stress levels, anxiety, and even depression. When we are constantly shifting our attention, our minds never get a chance to rest, eventually leading to burnout.

Have you ever had a day when you'd had enough of everyone and snapped? And nothing "major" set you off? That's what chronic multitasking does to us. It stretches us thin like a worn rubber band and makes us irritable, exhausted, and ineffective. We might look like we are busy, but inside, we are ready to unleash a sarcastic rant at the next person who asks us to juggle one more task. It does not matter if it's your manager at work, your partner at home, your kids just being kids or hell ... you could be sick of yourself! So forget what we have been taught about being able to multitask – it's a LIE!

Personal Anecdotes: Lessons from Dad

My dad had his own theories about multitasking, which he often shared in the form of colorful anecdotes. One of his favorites was about trying to catch two rabbits at once. "Shana," he'd say, "if you try to catch two rabbits at the same time, you'll end up with none." I used to laugh it off, but as I grew older and busier, his words began to resonate.

My dad is a man of many hats – literally and metaphorically. He knows everything about politics, sports, music, and, most important, people and the way they move. He is a self-taught multi-hyphenate who can build things, repair cars, and in general solve problems like a champion. Even with all this skill and talent, he believed in focusing on one task at a time and doing it well. "You cannot ride two horses with one behind," he'd chuckle, and I'd roll my eyes. But he was right. Trying to divide my attention meant that I wasn't truly present for any task.

The Modern-Day Busy Badge

You ever notice that you have that one friend who is always so busy? The one who wears their busyness like a badge of honor. We equate a packed schedule with importance and success. But just because we are busy does not mean we are productive. It reminds me of the franticness of online dating. One app never seemed like enough. I'd have two or three on my phone swiping mindlessly left and right; never really finding "the one." I kissed a lot of frogs but did not meet my prince that way. Time and time again I learned that busy is not the same as being effective.

And this is not just happening in our personal lives. It's also infected the workplace. Our cultural glorification of busyness leads to environments where employees feel compelled to be constantly "on."

The result? Burnout, stress, and a significant drop in actual productivity. Leaders who reward visible busyness rather than actual outcomes create a toxic work culture where the quality of work suffers. Think FaceTime, forced in-person meetings, and meetings that could have been an email. Ouch!

Being busy is a trauma response. When you are busy you do not have to deal with ANY of the mess you'd have to confront if you just slowed down. Keeping "busy" keeps us on the hamster wheel of life.

Recognizing the Costs of Busyness

The costs of busyness extend beyond the workplace, seeping into our personal lives, affecting our relationships and personal well-being. When was the last time you truly enjoyed a hobby without feeling guilty about not working? When did you last spend quality time with your loved ones without your mind wandering off to unfinished tasks? When was the last time you slowed down enough to spend time with YOU?

It's like trying to enjoy a slice of cheesecake with the girls while worrying about the calories – you miss the joy of the moment. The constant pressure to be busy robs us of these simple pleasures.

Strategies for Purposeful Productivity

So, how do we shift from busyness to purposeful productivity? Here are a few things that I go to time and time again that have helped me get back on track, and I believe they can help you, too:

- **Prioritize tasks:** Identify your most important tasks and focus on them. This means saying no to less critical activities, just as my mama would firmly say no to nonsense I wanted to do as a kid.

- **Time blocking:** Allocate specific times for different tasks and stick to it. Like setting aside an hour to enjoy *Bridgerton* without interruptions – pure bliss. Tee-hee!

- **Mindful decision-making:** Before committing to a task, ask yourself if it aligns with your goals and values. Is it necessary, or is it just adding to your busyness?

- **Set boundaries:** Learn to say no and protect your time. Imagine Sophia snapping, "No, I'm not doing that," and channel that energy.

- **Self-care:** Make time for rest and activities that rejuvenate you. Whether it's a walk in the park, a hobby, or simply watching your favorite TV show, prioritize self-care. I am going to talk more about this because I would be disappointed if you did not roll your eyes. Why? Because these are some of the tactics that have shown up in books on time management, organization, leadership, getting ahead, self-improvement ... you name it! I also think that even though we know what to do, we do not do it because we are rebelling against the idea that we need balance and rest to be successful.

The Golden Girls' *Wisdom*

The Golden Girls might have been ahead of their time when it comes to understanding the importance of meaningful connections and purposeful living. They laughed, cried, and navigated life's challenges together, always prioritizing their friendship over the hustle and bustle.

In many ways, they were the epitome of intentional living. Blanche embraced life's pleasures, Rose found joy in simplicity, Dorothy sought wisdom, and Sophia kept things real. They were not busy for the sake of being busy. They were purposeful, present, and always true to themselves. I'll share more lessons and antidotes that made me think and laugh throughout the rest of these pages. If you have not seen the show or need a quick primer, remember to flip to the end of the last chapter.

The Pursuit of Happiness: Beyond Busyness

Now, let us delve deeper into the pursuit of happiness and how it intertwines with our approach to productivity. Happiness is not just a fleeting emotion but a state of well-being that encompasses satisfaction with life, a sense of purpose, and positive relationships. My dad would say that happiness is fleeting and reminded me to focus on being content. But if I did not feel successful then how could I feel happy? And if I wasn't happy, how would I reach a state of contentment?

Research in positive psychology has shown that happiness is not achieved through constant activity but through meaningful engagement and connection. Dr. Martin Seligman, a leading figure in positive psychology,[3] introduced the PERMA model,[4] which outlines five elements that contribute to well-being: positive emotion, engagement, relationships, meaning, and accomplishment. I was super excited to happen on this body of research because I instinctively knew that I needed to pay closer attention to my emotions, my relationships, meaning, and accomplishments, which show up as purpose. But I did not have the lexicon to describe how that looked in real life outside of my own instincts.

The PERMA Method in Real Life

In discovering the PERMA method, one question continued to bother me. How do we move toward well-being when we are overwhelmed? In this section, I explain how the PERMA method works outside of textbooks and research papers. To do that, I flipped through journals I'd been keeping since my 20s to see if I'd ever made a concerted effort to embrace this approach to well-being.

Positive Emotion

One of my strengths is looking to the future and being able to imagine an outcome. And although that enabled me to cast a big vision, it did not leave space for me to enjoy the process leading up to that outcome. You know … the "now." Experiencing joy, gratitude, and contentment is essential for our overall happiness. However, when we are constantly busy, we often overlook these moments. Taking time to appreciate small joys, like a sunny day or a heartfelt conversation, can significantly enhance our well-being. I realized that when I slowed down just enough to smell the proverbial roses, that I wrote about how happy I was and how my day, even with some obstacles in the way, was awesome.

---

[3] Wagner (2018).

[4] Sutton, Jeremy. (2016). Martin Seligman's positive psychology theory. Positive Psychology. https://positivepsychology.com/positive-psychology-theory/

Engagement

My friends would describe me as a busy, creative person. I think they are too kind. Most days you'd find me phone in hand, texting my team and trying to clean while trying to have a phone conversation. Engagement, or being fully absorbed in activities, leads to a state of flow where we lose track of time and feel energized. This cannot be achieved through multitasking because our attention is divided. Instead, focusing on one task at a time enables us to experience deeper engagement and satisfaction. I recognized just how difficult it has been to do this. My mind often wandered, and I could tell it was a struggle at times for me to stay on course, even in my own writing.

Relationships

One of my life pillars is that we are in the "business" of relation-ships. It does not matter what type of industry you are in, what your profession is, or what part of the world you live, our real currency is relationships. Positive relationships are a cornerstone of happiness. When my relationships – familial, work, and romantic – are healthy and being nurtured, they thrive. When we are too busy, we neglect our relationships, leading to feelings of isolation and loneliness. Prioritizing time for loved ones and fostering meaningful connections can greatly enhance our sense of belonging and happiness. Simply put, that is bad for business.

Meaning

Having a sense of purpose and meaning in life is crucial for long-term happiness. Finding happiness is a universal human pursuit, but true, lasting happiness often stems from having a sense of meaning and purpose in life. When we are caught up in busyness, we lose sight of what truly matters. Imagine me, just doing "stuff" because I was told that that's what I am "supposed" to do. But this scenario is all too common, leaving many of us feeling unfulfilled and disconnected from our true selves. The key to breaking free from this cycle and cultivating genuine happiness lies in identifying and pursuing activities that resonate with our core values and provide a sense of purpose.

Journaling has kept me honest about what I want and helped me stay in the present on course toward my purpose. I define purpose as my values in action in this current season of my life. By being clear about my values and regularly documenting my thoughts, feelings, and experiences, I can gain valuable insights into what brings me joy and fulfillment. Journaling serves as my mirror, reflecting my inner world and helping me identify patterns in my emotions and behaviors. And it can work for you, too.

Accomplishment

Achieving our goals and feeling a sense of accomplishment boosts our self-esteem and happiness. However, it's important to set realistic goals and celebrate our successes along the way. Constant busyness without recognizing our achievements leads to burnout and dissatisfaction. Ooof! Sound familiar? When was the last time you paused to say, "I DID THAT"? Many of us spend more time talking crazy to ourselves about what we DIDN'T do. So, we keep going after more. Staying in a constant state of chasing accomplishments is an empty feeling, and the truth is we start filling that empty feeling with things (insert food, social media, shopping, travel, volunteering, etc.). I was filling my empty feeling with all these things! I never stopped and rarely slowed down. When I did slow down even a little bit, I realized that I never felt like I'd accomplished anything. So I'd start the race all over again. This is not sustainable, friend. And later I'll talk about how I paid the price for this constant state of "busy."

Breaking Free: Making Every Minute Matter

As I wrap up this chapter, I want to take a moment to reflect on the lessons learned. Why do we cling to our busyness badge with such fervor? In this book, I cover this as well as healthy strategies and tactics to get out of the high-occupancy-vehicle (HOV) lane of busy, but here are a few biggies:

- **Society glorifies busyness:** We see it everywhere – the "hustle culture" on social media, the crammed schedules of high-powered executives. It's easy to feel like if you are not constantly on the go, you are somehow falling behind.

- **Busyness can be a shield:** Sometimes, we use busyness to avoid dealing with more difficult things – unfinished projects, looming deadlines, or even just the need for some good old-fashioned self-reflection. Hey, it's easier to drown yourself in to-do lists than confront your fear of public speaking, right? (Although, let's be honest: even Blanche would struggle to write a compelling speech while simultaneously applying lipstick and wrangling a cheesecake.)

- **The busy trap is a sneaky one:** It can leave you feeling stressed, overwhelmed, and burnt out. It can damage your relationships, both personal and professional. And worst of all, it can steal your joy and leave you feeling like a hamster on a never-ending wheel.

- **Being busy is not the same as being productive:** Multitasking is not a badge of honor but a chain that binds us. It's time to break free from the myth of busyness and embrace a more intentional, purposeful approach to life.

There is a way out of the busy trap.

In the coming chapters, I explore strategies to accomplish the following:

- **Identify your priorities:** Not all tasks are created equal. Learn to differentiate between the mission-critical stuff and the tasks that can be delegated, automated, or (gasp!) eliminated altogether.

- **Embrace focus:** Multitasking is a myth. The human brain is wired for single-minded attention. By focusing on one task at a time, you'll get more done and with better quality (no more paint-splattered houses, Dad!).

- **Master your time:** Become a time ninja! Learn techniques like time blocking and setting boundaries to ensure you are using your precious minutes for what truly matters.

- **Prioritize self-care:** You cannot pour from an empty cup. Make time for sleep, exercise, and activities that bring you joy. A well-rested, happy you is a much more productive you (and a much more fun person to be around).

I want you to imagine a life where you are not constantly overwhelmed but focused and fulfilled. A life where your actions are driven by purpose, not by the need to be busy. Just like the beloved Golden Girls, let us strive for a life filled with laughter, meaningful connections, and purposeful actions.

Remember, this journey is about creating a life that works for you, not the other way around. It's about ditching the "busy badge" and embracing a more mindful, intentional approach to work and life. So, grab a beverage of your choice (rosé for the adventurous, cheesecake for the indecisive, a strong cup of coffee for the go-getters – we are all welcome here!), settle in, and let us get this party started!

CHAPTER 2

THE SANDS OF TIME ARE LITTERED WITH TO-DO LISTS

"My to-do list is so long that it doesn't have an end; it has an event horizon."

CRAIG BRUCE

Shana, when you are lazy, you are doing the work twice! That's what my dad would always holler at me growing up whenever he caught me taking a break from my chores or only putting as little effort as I could. Looking back, I realize now that was his own special brand of pushing me toward excellence – the art of scrutinizing every little detail to an infuriating degree so that I'd get it right the first time.

My dad is a Caribbean man who brought all those old-school island values with him to the States. You know the ones I'm talking about – that hardcore work ethic instilled by a childhood of living in the countryside – hard work, focus, discipline, and order, where idleness was considered a sin on par with the deadly variety. Bless his heart, my daddy just could not comprehend the concept of rest and relaxation.

"Shana, why put off for tomorrow what can be done tahday?" he'd bark in that thick Jamaican patois that could shred steel. "You tink money grows on trees? We nah have time fi dat!"

The Hustle of Single Motherhood

It's a minor miracle I did not develop a complex from constantly getting the side eye for the simple act of sitting down. Though I suppose that relentless drive did prepare me for what was to come – the endless hustle of single motherhood.

Because if there's one thing all my solo moms can agree on, it's that being a single mom leaves no time for chill mode. Especially when you are raising a strong-willed, quick tongued, funny as all get-out queenager like my daughter, Sanai.

Now as a rising sophomore at university, the queenager is the perfect intersection of Blanche Devereaux's brazenness and Sophia Petrillo's brutal honesty. She's got the confidence and swagger of a Queens girl who's ready to run the world, mixed with the unapologetic candor that can only come from the mouth of a kid who was heavily influenced by her Caribbean grandparents – who have seen it all.

"Mommy, why you always gotta make things so complicated?" she'll sigh, hands on hip in that iconic gesture of exasperated wisdom beyond her years. "You need to stop bein' all extra and just handle it, for real."

The queenager is the first to call out my tendency to overcomplicate even the simplest of tasks. To be fair, I come by my predisposition for doing the absolute most honestly – it's a core part of my Caribbean cultural DNA, passed down for generations like a genetic mutation. We island folks just cannot seem to help ourselves when it comes to overanalyzing and overdoing every little thing.

It's a compulsion fueled by childhood stories of time on the island, when my aunts and uncles had to stretch every dollar and not waste food. Scarcity is coded into our psychological blueprints, making us want to control and conserve every finite resource down to the most miniscule grain of sand.

So you can imagine the level of internal panic I experienced when I found myself having to be the sole provider and planner for every single aspect of my child's life. Suddenly, I was the one lugging the proverbial water to and from the well every day, all while trying to keep my head above the rising tides of solo parenthood.

In those early years, I was a walking, talking embodiment of stress – the human equivalent of being woken up by a car alarm going off at 3 a.m. in a quiet neighborhood. I micromanaged the heck out of every little detail in both our lives, desperate to retain some sense of control and order amidst the overwhelming chaos of divorce, moving across the country for a new role, and dealing with the financial and emotional fallout of my former well-planned life.

My obsessive planning and scrutinizing every decision I needed to make reached epic proportions, and no one could see it. I'd spend hours agonizing over the queenager's outfits and hairstyles, as if dressing her for the runway rather than third-grade recess. Making her lunch felt like a high-stakes cooking competition, with me fretting over whether the strawberries were sliced at the perfect thickness and the sandwiches cut into isosceles triangles rather than boring rectangles (I gave that mess up at the beginning of third grade).

Even the most mundane aspects of our daily routine were subject to my excessive oversight. I'd hover over the queenager while she brushed her teeth, watching with a critical eye to ensure she hit that full two-minute mark and did not miss a single molar. Bedtime was a whole production, with me spending a good half-hour fluffing pillows and fussing with her covers until they were tucked in at a precise 32° angle for optimal sleeping conditions.

"Mommy, you gotta chill!" the queenager would protest, swatting away my hovering hands. "I'm a big girl!" What was my excuse for driving myself and my kid crazy with my obsessive need to control every detail? I was a nervous wreck with an internal dialogue that screamed "You're already a failure as a wife so do not mess this up."

Well, my therapist would say it was rooted in my anxieties about being a single parent. With no partner to share the mental, physical, or financial load, I put the entire weight of planning and preparation on my own shoulders. I figured if I could just get every little thing perfect, it would somehow make up for the lack of a second parent and spare the queenager any sense of lack.

The Root of My Micromanaging

My dad, however, had a more … traditional take on my micromanaging tendencies. "You need to get a grip, Shana!" he'd chide me whenever he'd catch me fretting over something. He would talk to me about how I worried over "minor tings." So no matter what I had to do, I would just press on and not complain.

Ah yes, there's that classic immigrant parent logic that prioritizes productivity over all else. By their standards, unless you are breaking an actual sweat from physical labor, you are not working hard enough. Fight me on that. I said what I said.

"Back home, we could not just lollygag around worryin' "bout likkle tings," Dad would continue, a twinkle in his eyes and a smile on his face. "We had to just buckle down and get stuff done, ya kno? No time to coddle nobody or fuss over di likkle details!"

I'd just shake my head and chuckle, only half-listening to his usual rants about the good old days. Because as much as I loved my dad, his old-school mindset was part of the exact mentality I was trying to overcome – that misguided notion that constantly moving from one task to the next without a moment's pause was the key to true productivity.

My mom also had a particular way about doing things. The irony was, my mom's own management of our household when I was a kid was a big part of what instilled my own obsessive tendencies in the first place. I needed to be perfect. Things had to be "just so." I was representing my parents wherever I went and my parents knew … everyone!

I can still hear Mama Dawn's voice echoing through our apartment, bellowing things like, "Kishshana! Why you leave on all the lights? You tink money grows on trees?" "Why you sleeping?" Or "Let us GO; we have tings to do."

Looking back, I realize my mom's specificity came from that same place of scarcity hardwired into our Caribbean psyches. Even though she grew up with means, you would not know it. And let us not forget my dad, having grown up with literally nothing, he was terrified of anything going to waste – even that last tiny squeeze of toothpaste or the precise arrangement of our sofa cushions.

At the time, I just thought he was being a massive pain in the behind. But now I can have more empathy for where that obsessive attention to detail came from. My dad's micromanaging was his way of trying to retain control in a world where he'd had to fight tooth and nail just to survive.

Which, I suppose, is not so different from my own struggles as a single mom, constantly grasping for that same sense of order and stability. We're just two generations of Caribbeans trying to micromana-geour way to security, with varying degrees of success.

The Birth of the reTHINK Method

The difference, though, is that I eventually realized that approach was doing me more harm than good. I had no idea that all that obsessive planning and nitpicking was only serving to ramp up my anxiety, not alleviate it. I was exhausting myself by constantly swimming against the tide, rather than learning to ride the waves. And friend, I did not realize, accept, and DO anything about it until I hit the big 4-0.

That's when I knew I needed to reTHINK my entire approach to this whole #hustleculture lifestyle I'd bought into. Because despite what Caribbean (and other immigrant) cultural values claimed, there's absolutely nothing productive about running oneself into the ground with unnecessary stress in pursuit of someone else's idea of success.

Note: That's where my reTHINK method was born – a way to embrace thoughtful productivity without sacrificing my sanity. It's all about being more intentional in how I plan and move through life as a working single mom, stripping away the busywork and cutting out the noise so I can focus on what matters most.

The Five Core Principles of the reTHINK Method

I created the reTHINK method because it was clear that overcoming the pervasive culture of busyness would require more than just hard work – it would require smart work. I wanted to offer a systematic approach to leadership that emphasizes thoughtfulness over sheer effort, strategic rest over constant engagement, and overall wellness over temporary achievements.

I want you to lay the groundwork for transforming your life and leadership from a high-stress liability into a sustainable asset. By understanding the limitations of old ways of thinking and doing and the potential of new strategies, you'll be better equipped to navigate your roles with confidence and foresight. As a leader, this not only enhances organizational outcomes but also improves personal satisfaction – culminating in a leadership style that is as rewarding as it is effective and most importantly is you.

I challenge you to critically assess your current leadership styles and embrace innovative practices that align with the complexities of the workplace. This is an invitation to step out of comfort zones and lead with renewed purpose and insight.

R – Redefine Productivity

The first step is redefining what true productivity means, beyond just checking tasks off a never-ending to-do list. It's about working smarter, not harder – maximizing your output while minimizing unnecessary effort and stress.

For me, that means being more intentional about how I spend my limited time and energy. Instead of cramming in activity after activity, I've learned to schedule plenty of buffer room to rest, recharge, and actually enjoy some guilt-free leisure time. And let me tell you, that mess is HARD AF! The first few months I leaned into this for real, I thought I was losing it. I had anxiety attacks, night sweats, dry mouth, acne. And it wasn't just because I was newly perimenopausal. My inner Kish (I'll call her Tina) was not having it. All my life I'd been on the go. My third gear was someone else's sixth gear (or overdrive), and my sixth gear was like a super turbo charged-up muscle car ready to gooooooooooo. I could not find peace in the stillness of rest. I had to redefine my idea of rest to make it work for me.

I've also had to overcome that cultural conditioning that dismissed anything other than traditional labor as "not real work." Whether it's reading a book, taking a walk, or just zoning out on the couch for a bit, I've given myself full permission to engage in those restorative activities without feeling like I'm being "unproductive."

Because here's the truth – you'll never be as productive as you could be if you are constantly running on fumes. Hustling 24/7 with no breaks is a recipe for burnout, not success. Redefining productivity means working in a more sustainable way that avoids that catastrophic crash and burn.

E – Evaluate Your Priorities

Once you have redefined what productivity means for you, it's time to start evaluating what and who actually deserves your time and energy. Not every task is created equal, and it's important to be able to separate the busywork from your actual priorities.

This is where being a single mom has really forced me to hone those prioritization skills. With so little time and only one pair of hands, I've had to get ruthless about cutting out the excess and focusing only on the essentials for me and the queenager. When I did not … disaster.

For example, I've learned that although having a perfectly made bed is my standard, it's not a priority compared to making sure the queenager has a nutritious breakfast before school. Keeping an immaculately clean home is all well and good, but not when it comes at the expense of being present for quality time together after her classes (insert a monthly housekeeper).

It's about evaluating what really needs my limited bandwidth, and letting go of the rest without any guilt or second-guessing. Sure, those other tasks might get done eventually – but only once the mission-critical priorities are handled first.

T – Thoughtful Planning

This one is all about being more strategic and thoughtful in how you approach your planning and scheduling. No more just winging it or overloading your calendar with a million random tasks. It's about being more intentional in how you map out your time.

For me, this meant scheduling a weekly planning session to map out a high-level schedule for the queenager and me. I'd block off all the must-do events and obligations first – her track or swim meets, my work meetings, appointments, and so on. Then I'd layer in buffer times for transitions between activities, as well as scheduled pockets for meals, chores, and yes – rest and leisure. My calendar looks like Joseph's coat of many colors. Now that she's in college, I've had to find a new rhythm for myself. I'm not gonna lie, it's been tough settling into this new identity as an empty nester. I did not imagine I would struggle because I thought I was ready. Friend, I was w-r-o-n-g! I kept up with my weekly high-level review of my personal and professional schedule because I've found this type of scheduling to be a game changer. It enables me to see my availability at a glance and allocate my time more effectively, instead of just reactively cramming things in wherever I can. It's about being more proactive and thoughtful in how I use those 24 hours, rather than just blazing through each day in a frantic, frazzled mess. And I still share calendars with my kiddo and my team.

H – Holistic Perspective

In order to be truly productive in a sustainable way, you have to take a more holistic view that accounts for all aspects of your life – not just work or chores or parenting. It's about being more in tune with your overall mental, physical, and emotional needs.

For me, this has meant getting better about tuning into my body's signals before I'm running on those last dregs of energy. If I'm feeling depleted or rundown, I give myself full permission to take a break and recharge through exercise, meditation, or just some good old-fashioned vegging out on the couch.

It's also involved setting firmer boundaries to protect my time and energy. That meant getting better about saying no to extra commitments or obligations that will spread me too thin. It meant offloading more tasks and responsibilities to the queenager to develop her self-sufficiency before she went off to college. And it meant being more vocal about calling in reinforcements from friends and family when I needed an extra set of hands.

Because at the end of the day, I'm just one person – a human being with finite resources, not an inexhaustible machine that can just power through on grit alone. Taking a holistic view means respecting my limitations and working within them, not constantly trying to override them through sheer force of will.

I – Inclusive Mindset

Next up is having an inclusive mindset. This is about making sure my productivity philosophy works for everyone in my life – not just me. It's about bringing the queenager, my partner, and others into the process, instead of just imposing my personal systems on them.

For the queenager, that looks like getting her input on certain scheduling decisions that affect her. It has meant giving her more autonomy to manage her own time and responsibilities as she gets older. And it meant being more collaborative in how we divvy up chores and household tasks, taking her thoughts and preferences into account. I want y'all to know that I exasperated my parents with this style of parenting.

With my friends and family, it's meant being more transparent about my needs and limitations, so they understand where I'm coming from. It meant not being afraid to ask for help when I need it, and trusting that there are people in my life who want to support me. It's about building a network of mutual support, rather than trying to be a single-mom martyr who has to do everything alone. Oooooooh! Let me say that again! It's about building a GOOD network of mutual support (and getting rid of the energy vampires who suck on my time, my kindness, and create more fatigue).

Because, as much as I might want to, I cannot just unilaterally impose my reTHINK philosophy on the rest of the world. True productivity has to work for everyone involved, not just me. It's about finding that balance and compromise, and bringing an attitude of flexibility rather than rigid control.

Now I know what you might be thinking: "Damn, Kish – that's a whole lot of steps and introspection just to get stuff done! Why do you have to make productivity so complicated?"

N – Navigate Shifts

The *N* in reTHINK stands for navigating shifts in culture and values. As a single mom and Caribbean American, I've had to learn how to adapt to changing norms and expectations in my personal life and in the working world.

For example, the traditional values I was raised with often clash with modern parenting philosophies. Although my dad emphasized strict discipline and unquestioning obedience, I've had to find a middle ground that works for me and my own child. One that respects her autonomy and encourages open communication, while still maintaining clear boundaries and expectations.

At work, I've also had to navigate cultural shifts, especially as a Black woman in predominantly white corporate spaces. I had to find my own center lest I be swallowed whole by assimilation and code-switching. Early on I learned to adapt my communication style to be heard and respected, without compromising my authentic self. It's an ongoing balancing act. Navigating shifts is about being flexible and adaptable, while staying true to your core values. It's recognizing that change is constant, and being willing to roll with the punches as needed, even if it means rethinking long-held beliefs and approaches.

K – Know When to Pause

Finally, the *K* is all about knowing when to rest before you rush to reset. It's recognizing when you are reaching your limits and need to take a break before you completely burn out. As a chronic overachiever, this has been one of the hardest lessons for me to learn. I'm so conditioned to just power through, even when I'm running on fumes. I am relentless when my mind is made up. However, I've come to realize that rest is a crucial part of the productivity equation. You cannot pour from an empty cup.

So now, I make a point to schedule in regular breaks and downtime, even if it's just 10–15 minutes to stretch, hydrate, and regroup. I've learned to pay attention to my body's signals and respect when I need to slow down. Whether that's taking a mental health day off work, or asking my partner to take charge of dinner so I can decompress for a bit. Knowing when to pause is about having the self-awareness and discipline to prioritize rest and recovery. To recognize it not as "laziness" or "unproductive time," but as a strategic investment in your long-term performance and well-being. Put on your own oxygen mask first, as they say.

So there you have it – the full reTHINK model for achieving more by doing less. Redefine what productivity means for you, evaluate your true priorities, plan with intention, take a holistic view, be inclusive of others, navigate shifts with agility, and know when to hit pause. It's not about doing more, but doing what matters most, in a way that works for you and those around you. So you can stress less and accomplish more.

And if all else fails? Just ask yourself, "What would Sophia Petrillo do?" Guaranteed she'd find a way to get it handled while still making time for cheesecake. Because that's the real golden secret to a life well lived. Prioritize the sweetness, even amidst the chaos. Everything else will fall into place.

Anna's Story

I am not alone in my relentless pursuit of being an efficient multitasker. One of my clients told me her story of how she kept trying to get ahead with what I call "the 19 tabs open approach" and how it nearly put her in the hospital.

In the dim light of early morning, Anna sat at the small, cluttered desk that occupied a corner of her equally small apartment. Her gaze wandered from the computer screen to the window where the first hints of dawn painted a quiet cityscape. She had been up most of the night, her mind a battleground of competing tasks – a presentation due at 9 a.m., a mounting inbox of emails screaming for attention, and a research paper for her PhD that had not progressed beyond its abstract.

She had always prided herself on her ability to juggle multiple responsibilities. "Multitasking," she would say with a hint of bravado when friends expressed their astonishment at her workload. But lately, each ball seemed heavier, each throw more taxing than the last.

Her phone buzzed with an incoming message, snapping her back to reality. It was from Tom, her colleague who seemed perpetually calm amidst chaos. "Remember," he texted, "you got this. Also, close those tabs." She smiled wryly; even Tom had noticed her fraying edges.

As she turned back to her presentation, trying to channel Tom's advice, there was an unexpected knock on the door. She hesitated but decided to answer it: it was Mrs. Wallace from next door holding two large bags of groceries struggling slightly under their weight.

"Dear, could you lend me a hand with these for a moment?" Mrs. Wallace asked with a warm smile.

Helping her neighbor provided Anna with an unexpected pause from her digital tethers. As they arranged the groceries together in Mrs. Wallace's kitchen, Anna felt a strange sense of relief washing over her – a brief respite where only one task held her attention.

Returning to her apartment and sitting back down at the desk felt different now; there was clarity in simplicity she had not felt before. She closed all applications except for her presentation and began working through it slide by slide with renewed focus.

The sun climbed higher as morning turned into afternoon; light spilled across Anna's notes and highlighted words that seemed clearer now than they ever did while multitasking. A realization dawned on her: perhaps what she needed wasn't more hours in the day but rather more depth in each hour spent. Anna recounted this day trying to hold back tears. She was trying to get a promotion, was working her buns off to get her dissertation completed, and trying to date in New York City.

Could it be that our quest for efficiency through multitasking is actually leading us astray?

Unraveling the Myth of Multitasking

My story and Anna's story are not unique. In today's hyper-connected world, the allure of multitasking is more tempting than ever. However, the belief that juggling multiple tasks at once increases productivity is a pervasive myth. I gotta admit, I was in denial about this.

The Sands of Time Are Littered with To-Do Lists

I prided myself on the idea that I could do multiple things and do them well. So I want to dig in a bit on the cognitive limitations that make multitasking less efficient and explore why focusing on single tasks leads to better outcomes.

Multitasking is often celebrated as a skill of highly productive people, but research consistently shows it diminishes our cognitive abilities. When we split our attention, we extend the time needed to complete tasks and increase the likelihood of errors. Our brains are not wired to handle multiple tasks effectively. This realization can dramatically improve how we work and live.

The encouragement for multitasking stems from various cultural and workplace norms that equate busyness with productivity. I talked about a small part of how I was raised and how that created a foundation for doing "all the things." However, I needed to challenge these norms once I realized that **single-tasking not only speeds up work but also improves the quality of the outcomes**. By understanding the cognitive science behind focus and attention, you can begin to see why shifting away from multitasking can lead to more significant accomplishments.

Research That Redefines Productivity

Because I am a proud nerd, I looked to science to see if there were some key findings from cognitive psychology and neuroscience that underscore the benefits of the single-tasking approach. These insights are crucial for anyone looking to optimize their productivity in both personal and professional settings.

Extensive studies have shown that people who concentrate on one task at a time are not only more efficient but also experience less stress and greater satisfaction in their work. This is easier said than done. Shoot – I struggle with it at different parts of the year now! As a generalist, I like to have my hands in lots of things. But I use my method to restart without guilt. Letting go of the GUILT ... woosah I need to write a book about *that*.

Practical Steps Toward Focused Efficiency

Beyond just understanding the drawbacks of multitasking, I want to make sure you have concrete steps to cultivate a more focused workflow. You might have already tried techniques like the Pomodoro Technique to change workspace organization, and I explore a variety of methods that encourage deep work and minimize distractions. Each strategy is designed with real-world application in mind, ensuring you can implement these changes seamlessly into your daily routines. But behind the scenes, I want you to be thinking about what works *for you* and not what techniques the experts say you *should* do (that includes me, mmmmkay?)

Escaping the Busy Trap

These days, when everyone loves to brag about being busy, it's super important to realize that real productivity is all about being smart with how we use our energy. At work, leaders and managers can foster environments where employees are encouraged to thrive through focused effort rather than splintered attention. The transformation from multitasking to single-tasking is not just about personal efficiency; it's about cultivating a culture that values deep work and recognizes its impact on overall success.

Fun fact: multitasking can have detrimental effects on our mental well-being. Constantly switching between tasks can **increase stress levels** as we struggle to keep up with competing demands on our attention. The feeling of being overwhelmed by an endless list of responsibilities can lead to burnout and decreased job satisfaction. **Quality often falls victim to quantity** when we try to tackle too much at once. You know that feeling, right? It bubbles up in your stomach like one frank and beans serving too many on a hot summer day. You know that you do not have the space, time, or energy to add even one more thing to your plate and yet you do it anyway and then ... you get the productivity bubble guts!

Recognizing our limitations of multitasking is the first step toward reclaiming control over our productivity and well-being. By acknowledging that focusing on single tasks yields better results than attempting to juggle multiple responsibilities simultaneously, we can begin to **prioritize depth over breadth** in our work. Embracing a more intentional approach to self-management enables us to allocate our energy and attention more effectively, leading to improved outcomes and increased satisfaction with our achievements.

Multitasking and Hustle Culture Go Together Like a Jamaican Beef Patty and Coco Bread

One of my favorite things to do as a teenager was heading to the Coliseum Mall on Jamaica Avenue to get a beef patty with coco bread and cheese. The way the cheese melted perfectly into the patty and the hot cocoa bread gave a slightly sweet taste was perfection in an afternoon snack. Multitasking and hustle culture are also a perfect combination, but of struggle tears and deprivation.

Life's pretty crazy these days, right? With all the stuff fighting for our attention, it's easy to get pulled in a million directions. But here's the deal: there's something really special about putting all your energy into one thing at a time. It's like finding a secret superpower in the middle of all the noise! One of pop culture's favorite artists and entrepreneurs, Nipsey Hussle, proudly said that "I've been grinding all my life." Another icon and billionaire, Jay-Z, cemented this idea in a song whose lyrics proclaim, "I'm not afraid of dying, I'm afraid of not trying." So if some of our favorite artists, cultural stalwarts, and icons are heralding the benefits of being busy and modeling "do not stop until you are dead" behavior, how can you expect to escape this mentality and way of being? By committing fully to each task before moving on to the next, you can harness your mental energy more effectively and produce higher-quality outcomes in less time and with less energy. This approach not only benefits individual performance but also contributes to a more productive work environment overall.

When you prioritize single-tasking versus multitasking, you will be able to **deepen your concentration** on the task at hand. This depth of focus allows for greater creativity and problem-solving abilities, as well as an increased attention to detail that might be missed when attention is divided among multiple tasks simultaneously. For example, I got stuck writing a report for a client because I was also preparing for a conference I needed to submit my slides for, prepping for a committee meeting for my sorority chapter, and planning the next fundraiser for the parent teacher association at the queenager's school. Like – WHEEEEET??? I know you are nodding your head vigorously right now (or I just made you clench your bootie because how DARE me get in your head!?!).

But hear me out! By embracing the practice of single-tasking and dedicating focused blocks of time to each activity, you will actually start to love the things you do again. It'll give you an opportunity to move from a *routine-based approach* (read: I gotta do these five steps and then check it off my list) and move to a *ritual-based approach* (read: taking the time to move through each step and take special care during each). This shift in approach from multitasking to single-tasking might require a mindset adjustment initially, but it can lead to profound improvements in both professional performance and personal well-being over time. Here's a window into the five things that work for me:

- **One key strategy is to prioritize tasks** based on importance and urgency. By creating a clear plan of action and focusing on one task at a time, you can achieve better outcomes and avoid the pitfalls of trying to juggle multiple tasks simultaneously. Here's the rub. Many of us have been running on *E* for so long that we do not know where urgency begins and importance ends. We have not set boundaries with *ourselves* to make ourselves a priority. No wonder our busyness is giving us heart palpitations and heartburn. So, if **setting boundaries** is another vital technique for enhancing focus and efficiency, how do we begin to do that?

- **Establishing designated time blocks for specific tasks** helps in avoiding distractions and staying on track and should be the quick go-to response. By creating a structured schedule that allows for dedicated focus on each task, you can optimize that task's productivity and achieve better results. **Avoiding the temptation to switch between tasks** can lead to deeper concentration and higher-quality work. I use tools that block my distractions and give me allocated time for when I can do those things I want to by myself *instead* of just getting stuff done. But even if you are good at doing that (for a week or two) you struggle with maintaining this over time. Focus – 0. Distractions – 1.

- **Incorporating regular breaks** into your work and home routine is essential for maintaining focus and preventing burnout. Short breaks between tasks can help recharge the mind and improve overall productivity. By allowing time for rest and rejuvenation, you can approach each task with renewed energy and clarity. **Practicing mindfulness** during these breaks can further enhance focus and reduce stress levels, leading to improved performance. If you are looking for ideas on how to start a mindfulness practice as a reformed busybody, go to www.busyisafourletterword.com and download the "Busy Bee's Cheat Sheet to Mindfulness."

- **Using technology wisely** is another key aspect of avoiding multitasking. Although technology offers numerous benefits, it can also be a source of distractions. Setting boundaries with technology use, such as turning off notifications during focused work periods, can significantly improve concentration levels. **Implementing tools** like time management apps or website blockers can also help in minimizing distractions and boosting productivity. You might jump out of your seat on this one but for about three years I took email completely off my phone. Yep, I sure did! Although it made me have constant panic attacks for about a week, after a week I realized that anyone who needed me could actually get to me. And because I wasn't constantly being distracted by the ping of a new message everywhere I went, I felt more productive and centered and mostly calm.

- Have you ever walked into a colleague's office, or your high schooler's room, and the mess makes you dizzy? How could they accomplish ANYTHING in there? I'd always get the same response to my question: I know where everything is! **Creating a conducive work environment** is paramount to enhancing focus and efficiency. Research has shown that the cleanliness of your workspace can have significant effects on your productivity, behavior, and creativity. A study published in *Psychological Science*[1] found that working in a clean, orderly environment led to more conventional thinking and socially desirable behaviors, such as increased generosity and healthy eating choices. A tidy environment might encourage productivity in routine tasks. A clutter-free workspace with minimal distractions can foster a sense of calm and concen-

---

[1] Vohs, K. D., Redden, J. P., & Rahinel, R. (2013). Physical order produces healthy choices, generosity, and conventionality, whereas disorder produces creativity. *Psychological Science*, *24*(9), 1860–1867.

tration. By organizing work materials and eliminating unnecessary items, you can create an environment that promotes productivity and sharp focus. But never fear, my creative souls! A certain level of disorder might be beneficial for tasks requiring creative problem-solving and unconventional thinking. **Incorporating elements of nature**, such as plants or natural light, can also enhance cognitive function and overall well-being.

Practicing single-tasking as a deliberate approach to work can yield significant benefits in terms of productivity and quality of output. By dedicating full attention to one task at a time, you can complete tasks more efficiently and effectively. **Embracing the mindset** of focusing on one thing at a time not only improves task completion rates but also reduces stress levels associated with trying to do too much at once.

Four Steps to Ditching the Madness of Multitasking

Now I know I've given you all the things you are "supposed" to do. But we aren't robots and let us face it: life comes at you fast! There are the societal norms we are pressured to follow (who made these darn rules anyway), and then there are human-centered norms that take in account that we are not perfect. Here's what I mean:

- **Societal goal:** Improve productivity and efficiency by eliminating multitasking and fostering single-task focus.
- **Human-centered goal:** Slow down to enjoy life while doing the things that need to be done and the things that you want to do.

Recognize the Drawbacks of Multitasking

- Understand that multitasking leads to reduced productivity due to cognitive-switching costs.

- Realize how societal pressures push us toward multitasking despite its inefficiencies.
- Example: consider how frequently checking emails while working on a project results in slower progress and more mistakes.

Understand the Benefits of Focusing on Single Tasks

- Acknowledge improved quality of work when focusing solely on one task.
- Highlight increased creativity and deeper cognitive engagement through single-task focus.
- Notice when you cannot actually stay on task. There might be other factors at play.

Implement Techniques to Enhance Focus

- Create distraction-free environments by setting specific times for communication checks.
- Use time-blocking techniques: allocate dedicated periods for specific tasks.
- Prioritize tasks based on importance and break down larger projects into smaller steps.

Practice Mindfulness in Daily Tasks

- Emphasize being fully present in each activity you undertake.
- Incorporate mindfulness exercises like deep breathing or body scans before starting tasks.
- Recognize the reduction in stress levels and improvement in mental clarity through mindful practices.

The Sands of Time Are Littered with To-Do Lists

Conclusion: Breaking Free from the Busy Trap

Wooooosah. Friends, I know that was a lot! It might be time to take a quick break to let some of this sink in and reevaluate your environment and how you get things done. In the meantime, if you want the Cliffs Notes version, just remember this:

- My reTHINK method is all about being more thoughtful in how you work, more selective in what you prioritize, and more sustainable in how you approach your hustle.

- It's the antidote to that misguided "sleep when you are dead" grind culture that has us all burned out and depleted. It's about working smarter, not harder – getting more done by doing less, but doing it in a more strategic, energy-efficient way.

- So say it with me: *"Busy is a four-letter word that has no place in my vocabulary. My new philosophy is all about being productive with purpose."*

Now if you'll excuse me, I have a very important appointment to keep – with my sofa and a good book. Because even badass single moms like me need a break sometimes. Doctors' orders. I think I've earned the right to put my feet up and just … breathe. That is until I write the next chapter! Ready? Let us go!

CHAPTER 3

FROM ACTIVITY TO ACHIEVEMENT
CUTTING THROUGH THE CLUTTER

"I'm not saying I'm Wonder Woman, I'm just saying no one has ever seen me and Wonder Woman in the same room together."

UNKNOWN

Picture it: Sicily, 1922. If you have ever seen *The Golden Girls*, you know that Blanche, Dorothy, Rose, and Sophia had a knack for turning even the most mundane events into legendary tales. Much like them, our lives can often feel like a sitcom episode – filled with unexpected twists, hilarious mishaps, and the occasional heartfelt moment. Navigating these moments with thoughtful planning can make all the difference.

This chapter dives into the first pillar of the reTHINK method: **thoughtful planning before you move.** It's about creating detailed, reflective plans that align resources with goals, ensuring efforts are purposeful and effective. But do not worry, we'll keep it lighthearted and fun – because if Blanche taught us anything, it's that life's too short to take too seriously.

The Futility of Micromanaging Life

Let us face it, trying to micromanage every grain of sand in the hourglass of life is about as productive as Dorothy trying to teach Blanche how to be modest. Remember the episode where Dorothy attempts to manage Blanche's date schedule only to find herself entangled in a web of Southern charm and miscommunication? It's a classic example of how micromanagement can lead to chaos rather than control.

Instead of obsessing over every tiny detail, the key is to focus on the bigger picture – the strategic planning that helps you steer your life in the right direction without getting bogged down by minutiae. Think of it as planning your week like a *Golden Girls* episode: outline the main plot points, but leave room for spontaneous moments and unexpected laughs.

Maria's Story

The sun hung low in the sky, casting long shadows across the cobblestone streets of the small coastal town. Maria walked briskly, her mind a whirlpool of thoughts and emotions. She had spent the better part of her morning attending meetings that felt more like endless loops of rhetoric than anything productive. Each step she took seemed to echo the nagging question in her mind: was she truly accomplishing something meaningful or was she merely busy?

Her shoes clicked against the stones as she passed by a bakery. The scent of freshly baked bread filled the air, but Maria barely noticed. Her thoughts were consumed by an email from her manager that morning, requesting another report on a project that seemed to go nowhere. She had always prided herself on being efficient, but lately, efficiency felt like a mask for futility.

She paused at a crosswalk, watching cars rush by. The hum of engines and murmur of distant conversations enveloped her. Maria thought back to simpler times when her goals were clearer – when she wanted to write a novel that spoke to people's hearts or volunteer at shelters where she felt needed. Now, it seemed her days were filled with tasks that only served to keep her occupied rather than fulfilled.

As she continued walking toward the park where she usually found solace, Maria's phone buzzed with yet another notification – a reminder for an upcoming meeting about streamlining office procedures. She sighed and silenced it without looking at the details. The guilt gnawed at her; saying no felt like admitting failure, yet saying yes meant drowning further in meaningless activity.

The park offered some respite with its greenery and chirping birds creating a symphony around her. She found an empty bench and sat down heavily, staring at children playing tag nearby. Their laughter was infectious but also painful – a stark contrast to the weight she carried inside.

Maria closed her eyes for a moment and breathed deeply, trying to remember what true accomplishment felt like – the satisfaction that came from doing something aligned with one's values and aspirations. Could she trim away these unnecessary activities without losing herself in guilt? How could one find balance between obligations and meaningful achievements?

Are You Achieving or Just Staying Busy?

Maria's story is my story. I'd bet it's your story as well. In today's fast-paced world, being busy is often mistaken for being productive. Yet, merely filling our schedules with activities does not equate to achieving meaningful goals. We do not often make the distinction between activity and accomplishment; we need to emphasize that **prioritizing achievements over tasks is crucial for sustainable success.** That makes it easier to cut through the clutter to focus on what truly matters.

Busywork often consumes valuable time and energy, leading to exhaustion without significant progress. Americans work longer hours than ever before but feel less accomplished. The key lies in shifting focus from quantity to quality – allocating time and resources toward endeavors that align with personal and professional aspirations.

Distinguishing Between Activity and Accomplishment

The first step in combating the culture of busyness is understanding the difference between mere activity and true accomplishment. *Activities* are tasks that fill up your day but might not contribute significantly to your long-term goals. By contrast, *accomplishments* are milestones that bring you closer to your desired outcomes. For example, attending meetings might be necessary, but delivering a successful project is an accomplishment.

The Power of Saying No

Learn to decline with the grace of a Southern belle dodging suitors at a debutante ball. Okay. Confession. I struggle with saying no. I DO! Sometimes the guilt is so overwhelming it sounds like a loud alarm in my ear. I say yes to the brunch even though I want to sleep. I say yes to the project even though I do not like the work. I say yes to running errands for other people I would not say yes for myself. Eek! So what happens to my schedule? It looks like a clown car and I just tried to stuff one more thing in. I know better and I struggle anyway so I went in search of tools that would help me learn to say NO – a skill many struggle with due to the guilt associated with disappointing others. However, saying no is essential for protecting your time and energy. A study by University of California researchers found that people who struggle to say no are more likely to experience stress, burnout, and even depression.[1] Queue stress, burnout, and depressive episodes that crept up on me like a mist.

One practical approach is adopting a **value-based decision-making** process. By aligning your choices with your core values and long-term objectives, you can more easily identify which tasks deserve your attention and which do not. This method not only helps manage guilt but also fosters a sense of purpose and intention in your daily actions. Getting clear on my values – my Black Sheep Values[2] – helped me to identify what I really cared about when no one was looking. Doing so enabled me to run my options for what I

---

[1] World Health Organization. (2019, May 28). Burnout an "occupational phenomenon": International Classification of Diseases. https://www.who.int/news/item/28-05-2019-burn-out-an-occupational-phenomenon-international-classification-of-diseases

[2] Menswar, Brent. (n.d.). Discover your non-negotiables. https://www.brantmenswar.com/valuesassessment

wanted to do and what I felt obligated to do through that same filter. It took some time because I realized that I'd been operating for a really long time under the thumb of values that were not really mine. They were my parents' values, and I had to figure out FOR MYSELF what mattered to me.

Streamlining Efforts Toward Meaningful Goals

Developing a practice for evaluating and streamlining efforts toward meaningful goals involves regular reflection and adjustment. Start by setting clear, specific goals that reflect your values and aspirations. Break these goals into manageable steps and continuously assess whether your daily activities contribute toward them. I do not create more than three of anything. Not just because it's my favorite number, but I've learned as I get older, I am not holding more than three priorities front and center in my brain so it makes no sense to add more. So what are some goals that have previously felt like wishes? Like "maybe one day" type ideas you do not plan to get to because *where are you gonna to find the time?* I'm not gonna lie; I really felt like I was lost. Except I did not exactly know in what way and I really did not know what I would do if I was found. Getting clear on my values and being honest with myself about my priorities was critical.

Practical Tips for Implementation

Think of someone you admire who always seems to get stuff DONE. Instead of guessing what they do, ask them. What works for someone else might not work for you, but sometimes we need visual examples as a starting point. I like to approach implementation in large chunks. One of my best friends likes to break those chunks into smaller bites. Another colleague likes to see the whole layout and then, as long as there does not need to be an order of operations,

From Activity to Achievement: Cutting Through the Clutter

picks the hard things first to get them out of the way. What do all three of us have in common? Emphasizing quality over quantity, which allows for deeper engagement with work and personal pursuits alike.

Learning to say no is not a sign of weakness but rather a demonstration of strength and self-awareness. It's about honoring your priorities and commitments, both to yourself and others. By being selective about where you invest your time and energy, you create space for growth, creativity, and fulfillment.

Guilt often arises when we feel like we are letting others down by saying no. **However, setting boundaries is an act of self-care** that ultimately benefits everyone involved. When you say no to tasks that do not align with your goals, you are freeing up space to excel in areas where you can make the most significant impact. By declining activities that do not serve one's higher purpose, individuals create space for meaningful contributions and personal growth. This practice fosters a sense of agency and empowerment, enabling individuals to take control of their schedules and prioritize what truly matters.

In a world filled with constant demands and distractions, it can be challenging to differentiate between mere activity and true accomplishment. The distinction lies in the impact and value that each task brings to your life. *Mere activities* often keep us busy without moving us closer to our goals or fulfilling our deeper aspirations. However, *true accomplishments* are meaningful achievements that align with our values and contribute to our overall well-being.

Finding balance between obligations and aspirations requires **self-awareness** and clarity about one's values. When faced with multiple demands, it's essential to pause and reflect on whether each task aligns with overarching goals. This deliberate approach helps in discerning between activities that add value and those that merely contribute to the culture of busyness.

It's crucial to assess whether the tasks we engage in are simply keeping us occupied or if they are propelling us toward our desired outcomes. Activities can consume our time and energy, leaving us feeling drained and unfulfilled, while accomplishments bring a sense of purpose and satisfaction. By focusing on meaningful goals and prioritizing tasks that truly matter, we can shift from a state of busyness to one of productivity and fulfillment.

I cannot say this enough. **Learning to say no without guilt is a skill that requires practice and patience.** And when patience was being handed out, I am pretty sure I went to the bathroom. I do not have it! To say no without guilt involves setting clear boundaries, communicating assertively, and honoring one's priorities without apology. Over time, this practice becomes liberating, enabling individuals to invest their resources where they can make the most significant impact personally and professionally.

Pro Tip: You are not going to be able to sidestep the uncomfortable phase of taking back the control of your time, energy, and priorities. Your team members, colleagues, family members, and friends have an idea of you and when you decide to shift that idea, some folks are going to protest LOUDLY. This is where you are going to have to dig deep and focus on your ultimate goal: doing less.

This all sounds good in theory but day to day, **the key lies in understanding the purpose behind each task we undertake.** Are we engaging in activities out of habit or societal pressure, or are we intentionally working toward meaningful achievements? By cultivating this awareness, we can start to make conscious choices about how we invest our time and energy, moving away from busyness toward a more purposeful way of living.

47

From Activity to Achievement: Cutting Through the Clutter

Embracing Simplicity in Leadership

Lessons from African Traditions

Incorporating simplicity in leadership, inspired by African traditions, can transform organizational culture and effectiveness. Here are some practical ways to achieve this:

Emphasize Humility and Balance

- **Humility in leadership:** African leadership often emphasizes humility. Leaders should focus on serving their teams rather than exerting authority. This approach fosters respect and collaboration.

- **Balance and harmony:** The Yoruba concept of "Iwa Pele" (gentle character) stresses the importance of balance and harmony in decision-making. Leaders should strive to create a balanced work environment where all team members feel valued and heard.

Use Storytelling and Clear Communication

- **Storytelling:** Drawing from the rich tradition of African storytelling, leaders can use narratives to convey complex ideas simply and effectively. Stories can illustrate values, goals, and lessons in a relatable way, making the message stick.

- **Clear communication:** Simplifying communication is crucial. Leaders should distill information to its essential points and communicate them clearly. This reduces misunderstandings and ensures everyone is on the same page.

Simplify Strategies and Schedules

- **Strategic simplification:** Leaders should focus on simplifying strategies and goals. By eliminating unnecessary complexity, leaders can provide clear direction and make it easier for teams to align their efforts with organizational objectives.

- **Streamlined schedules:** Simplifying schedules helps prioritize essential tasks and reduces the clutter that can overwhelm teams. This approach enhances productivity and reduces stress.

Promote Transparency and Collective Decision-Making

- **Transparency:** African leadership values transparency and accountability. Leaders should be open about their decisions and processes, fostering trust within the team.

- **Collective decision-making:** Emphasizing group solidarity and collective decision-making can lead to more inclusive and well-rounded outcomes. Involving team members in the decision-making process ensures diverse perspectives are considered, leading to better solutions.

Foster a Culture of Simplicity

- **Cultural integration:** Embedding simplicity into the organizational culture requires consistent effort. Leaders should model simplicity in their actions and decisions, encouraging their teams to do the same.

- **Continuous improvement:** Organizations should regularly evaluate their processes and eliminate unnecessary complexity. This ongoing commitment to simplicity can drive long-term success.

By incorporating these principles inspired by African traditions, leaders can create a more effective, inclusive, and harmonious work environment. Embracing simplicity not only enhances productivity but also fosters a culture where every team member feels valued and empowered.

Thoughtful Planning Before You Move: A Reflective Approach

Have you ever watched an eight-year-old plan their day? It's a chaotic blend of homework, playtime, snacks, and an endless array of questions. As a precocious eight-year-old, I had a unique approach to time management that involved a lot of sticky notes and a relentless pursuit of fun. Here are some lessons from my younger self that still hold true when thoughtfully planning:

- **Prioritize playtime:** Just as kids know the importance of recess, adults need to prioritize downtime. Scheduling breaks and moments of joy can boost productivity and creativity. It's important to say that play is not just an activity but is treated as a state of mind. It is allowing yourself to lean into the joy of being and not just the constant state of doing.

- **Ask questions:** Never stop questioning why you are doing something. Is it necessary? Does it align with your goals? Just as I questioned the necessity of bedtime, question the necessity of tasks that do not contribute to your overall objectives.

- **Keep it simple:** Kids simplify everything. They focus on the immediate task at hand rather than overcomplicating things. Time to eat? They eat. Time to play. Focused. Apply this simplicity to your planning – focus on what needs to be done now and let future tasks wait their turn.

Strategic (Thoughtful) Planning: Aligning Your Daily Efforts with Bigger Goals

Thoughtful planning starts with a deep understanding of your goals and the resources at your disposal. You assess your situations thoughtfully before making a move. When you are busy, you are distracted, detached from what matters to you, and easily distressed when things do not go as planned. I've always been the kind of student to learn the rules and then break them. So in order to pressure test if my simplified method of thoughtful planning before I move (or make decisions) would work for anyone but me, I went to the text.

Y'all there are 1,687 methodologies for how to declutter your mind, prioritize your work and life, and become a more actualized human in the process. My challenge? They all put me to sleep. I just did not feel like they were designed for me – a high-achieving, multi-hyphenate CEO and solo mama who wanted to change the world one everyday leader at a time. So I remixed one of my favorites, the process model for prioritization and focus (PMPF).[3] This is how I ensure my plans are both reflective and effective.

I Reflect on My Goals

Typically, I start by defining what I want to achieve. I reflect deeply on my long-term goals and break them down into smaller, manageable tasks. This reflective approach ensures that each step I take is aligned with my overall vision. I have run away screaming from my whiteboard when writing down what I really want long term. Sometimes it was because I was so far down the road on one set of goals (even if those goals were not mine). Other times it was because I did not think I had the freedom to pivot because rent was due. Swim team fees were due. And people were counting on me. Damn, that's a lot of pressure for someone who was already a people-pleasing, high achiever prone to self-sabotage. OUCH!! But, I ate my Wheaties and got my courage and here we are!

---

[3] Scott, L. (2021). The savvy PMO's guide to prioritization. PMO Professionals.

From Activity to Achievement: Cutting Through the Clutter

I Assess My Resources

Next, I evaluate the resources available to me, be it time, money, or energy. Much like Blanche assessing her wardrobe before a date, knowing what I have helps me plan realistically and avoid overcommitment. Because I was typically "available" for everyone else, I assumed that when I needed support, folks would be there for me. Oh, friends, I got my feelings hurt more than once and more times than I care to recount. So I had to take stock of my true resources in order to make decisions that did not leave me empty, angry, or exhausted.

I Create a Flexible Plan

Life is unpredictable, and plans should be flexible enough to accommodate changes. I think of my plan as a *Golden Girls* episode – I know the main plot, but leave room for subplots and spontaneous moments that add to the richness of the story. This has helped me in many ways. One of my strengths is being strategic, and at its most simple idea that just means *there is always a better way*. I think about places I'd be willing to go with the flow and parts of my plan you'd have to pry from my cold, dead hands. This enables me to retain the control I need while making space for the unintended, unplanned, and unexpected.

The Importance of Rest: Knowing When to Pause

All this planning might do the opposite of what I want for you – ease while achieving more. Here's where I had to learn a new skill that even the Golden Girls knew the value of: a good rest. Remember the episodes where they'd sit around the kitchen table, late at night, sharing cheesecake and stories? People assume that rest equals sleep but those moments of rest and reflection in community are crucial for recharging and gaining perspective. This section explains three things I always do when thoughtfully planning.

I Schedule Downtime

I incorporate regular breaks and downtime into my schedule. Do not let me fool you, my schedule is still full. This is not just about physical rest but mental and emotional rejuvenation as well. Like Rose's St. Olaf stories, sometimes you need a break to gain a fresh perspective. Downtime for me is reading a novel, watching one of my favorite shows under the covers with my phone off, going for a walk or to a good Pilates session. I also shop in my downtime (oh, goodness, I have stories about *this)* and really think I have an un-tapped talent as a personal shopper for others. I really love it!

I Reflect and Adjust

I also use my downtime to reflect on my progress and adjust my plans if necessary. I've learned that making time for reflection helps me stay aligned with my goals and ensures that my actions remain purposeful.

I Embrace Unproductivity

This one is a tough one, friends. This one is a tough one because I grew up with this belief: **no idleness, no laziness, no procrastination: never put off tomorrow what you can do today**. However (*with clenched teeth*), not every moment needs to be productive. I am getting more comfortable with the reality that embracing unpro-ductivity is a necessary part of my creative and planning process. It's during these moments of "doing nothing" that some of the best ideas and insights often emerge.

Conclusion: From Planning to Purpose

Thoughtful planning is about more than just organizing tasks; it's about aligning your efforts with your goals and values. It's about finding balance, embracing flexibility, and knowing when to rest. As I've learned from *The Golden Girls*, life is full of unexpected moments and hilarity – but with thoughtful planning, you can navigate these moments with grace and purpose.

So, channel your inner Dorothy, Blanche, Rose, or Sophia – whichever Golden Girl resonates with you – and start planning thoughtfully before you move. Remember, it's not about micromanaging every detail but about creating a road map that guides you toward meaningful accomplishments.

As you continue to explore the reTHINK method, keep this chapter in mind. Thoughtful planning is the foundation that supports all other aspects of your journey toward achieving your goals. And always, always make room for cheesecake.

CHAPTER 4

CHECK UP BEFORE YOU CHARGE UP

HEALTHY ASSESSMENT BEFORE YOU ACT (reTHINK)

"I'm not procrastinating. I'm prioritizing."

JESSICA DAY, NEW GIRL

It's a sweltering summer day in Queens, and the sun is turning my living room into a scene from *The Golden Girls*. No, seriously. The fan is blowing hot air around, and I'm sipping iced tea, channeling my inner Blanche while attempting to juggle my to-do list like I'm still a student at Hillman College from *A Different World*. Somewhere between drafting a proposal and organizing a summer party for my daughter, I realize I've got to pause and take stock. If I'm going to make it through this week (and life, in general), I needed a solid game plan. I realized I'd just been "doing stuff." The essence of achieving more by doing less lies not in how packed your schedule is, but in how wisely you use your available resources.

The journey toward efficient resource management begins with understanding what you truly have at your disposal. It's easy to overestimate one's capacity and capabilities, leading to strategies that are not just unrealistic but also unsustainable. This chapter outlines methods to accurately gauge your personal and professional assets, which will serve as a foundation for informed decision-making. Recognizing the limits and potentials can dramatically shift how you approach tasks and goals.

I explore various tools and techniques that aid in making decisions grounded in reality rather than aspiration alone. These tools are designed to enhance cognitive processes, allowing for a clearer view of the practical implications of each decision. By prioritizing cognitive clarity, you position yourself to make choices that are not only ideal in theory but also executable in practice.

This chapter is about taking a healthy assessment of your resources, assets, and potential blind spots before you dive headfirst into any venture. The allure of ambitious projects is undeniable; however, without a grounded strategy, these projects can quickly lead to overcommitment and eventual burnout. I examine frameworks that help align ambitions with actual capabilities, ensuring that your energy is invested in pursuits that are both meaningful and manageable. Whether you are managing a household, running a

Check Up Before You Charge Up (reTHINK)

business, or both (like me), understanding what you have and what you are missing is crucial.

Let us get into it, because I have a feeling that this might hit home for you, especially if you grew up with negative reinforcement that encouraged you to work on your weaknesses and constantly strive for self-improvement as your North Star.

Are You Truly Leveraging Your Resources or Just Busy Being Busy?

When my dad retired about 10 years ago, he was going to get a "retirement job." Now you might be asking why would a fresh retiree want a job? My dad had been working since he was in single digits. From cutting, hauling, and selling sugar cane with one of his brothers to earn money for his family back home in Jamaica, to working two full time jobs with 1.5 days off a week most of my childhood, to working a third shift for 20 years and getting four hours or less sleep a day so he could shuttle my youngest sister around to her numerous activities until she went to college, he'd been a busy man. He was going to go from "too busy to think" to "way too much time" to think. So, his chill mode was getting a job driving a school bus to get him out of the house in the morning.

What he got was a not-so-chill job of stepping in to provide full-time cover for me when I suddenly found myself divorced with a toddler underfoot. As I zipped across the country every week, hustling to donor meetings and managing a national team at work while trying to be a super mom at home, dad was there to help me shoulder the huge responsibility as a solo mama. He knew what I did not. After years of being whirlwind busy, my dad leveraged decades of experience to slow down enough to focus on my kiddo so I could focus on rebuilding my shattered life. He warned that if I wasn't careful, I would run myself into the ground. Even armed with this much wisdom, it took years to slow down enough to understand why he wanted me to pace myself. It's critical to step back and evaluate whether this busyness is effective or merely a whirlwind of mind-numbing activity.

Embrace Practicality to Enhance Productivity

A common mistake in resource assessment is overlooking the human element – yourself. Acknowledging personal limits is crucial in setting realistic expectations and achieving sustainable success. I want to shout this from the mountain tops: your self-awareness is a significant component in resource allocation and how it prevents the common pitfall of overextension. It's critical to set the stage for success by starting with an honest appraisal of what is truly available to you – be it time, talent, or technology. Through strategic planning grounded in reality, you can transform the traditional notion of busyness from a passive state of being to an active pursuit of effectiveness.

The Importance of a Healthy Assessment

Busy is a four-letter word that society often equates with being successful, important, and necessary. But as my girl Dorothy Zbornak would say, "That's baloney!" Busyness without direction is just stress in disguise. And baaaaaybeeee; I had about 50-11 costumes. It was B-U-S-Y cosplay! I am an activator so I love to just GO but I have learned the hard way that although it might work to get something going, you'll lose air quickly. Kind of like the mysterious holes that always seem to be present in an air mattress. You lay down and the mattress is fully inflated but when you wake up you are lying flat on the ground.

I have to be really disciplined to ensure that before jumping into any project, I take a step back and realistically assess my resources. It does not hurt that I have a fantastic right hand at my company ManageMint, who keeps me in line and makes sure I stay focused. Blythe plays no games with me or about me, and I am grateful to have her running this race right alongside me. If I quiet my mind enough, I giggle when I think about watching my mom as a small child get ready for a night out. She would not just throw on any old thing and hope for the best. No, she'd assess her wardrobe, choose the perfect outfit, and make sure everything was on point. When she walked out the front door, she knew she was prepared for whatever the night air carried her way *and* she would look amazing! Similarly, you need to evaluate what you have at your disposal – time, money, skills, support systems – before committing to a new project.

Personal Anecdote
My Cozy Sanctuary

As a solo mom and the oldest in my family, I've often felt the weight of the world on my shoulders. For years, I rented a home that did not have consistent working heat. Yes, you read that right. Winters were rough, but I managed to make that house a cozy, warm, beautiful space that friends and family loved to visit. How? By assessing what I had and working creatively with it.

I knew my limitations – limited funds – but had a strong community and a knack for DIY and creative thinking. I used room heaters, online tutorials on keeping cold air out, Pinterest, and sheer willpower to transform my home. I did not focus on what I lacked (consistent central heating and money to purchase my own home); instead, I maximized what I had (lots of blankets, space heaters, style, and plenty of hot cocoa).

Self-Improvement Versus Asset Amplification

Our culture is obsessed with self-improvement, but this hyper-fixation can blind us to the assets we already have. Instead of constantly striving to improve, take a moment to acknowledge, amplify, and activate your existing strengths.

When I focused on making my home cozy despite its flaws, I wasn't fixated on the lack of heat. Instead, I amplified what I had – a knack for creating a warm atmosphere – and that skill made all the difference. Recognize your existing assets and use them to your advantage.

Steps for Conducting a Healthy Assessment

I did not have language at the time for how I made it work or how I managed to stay positive despite the stress, cold, and frequent inconvenience. But I realized I had a pretty consistent way that I looked at every situation, and it helped me to see possibilities where there did not seem to be any. Here's how I do it, and now you can, too:

1. **Inventory your resources:** Start by listing all your available resources. This includes tangible assets like money and tools, and intangible ones like skills, energy, and support systems. For example, if you are planning to start a business, assess your financial situation, your skill set, and your network. If you are a new caregiver, who in your support network would be willing to be a backup for you if you need it?

> **PSA:** And for those of you who do not like to ask people for help; stop it right now! It's killing you. Literally.

2. **Identify your strengths and blind spots:** Be honest with yourself about what you are good at and where you need help. For instance, Blanche knew her strength was her charm, but she'd also rely on Dorothy's wisdom or Rose's kindness when needed. In my own life, I know that I am quick with ideas and able to cast big visions. I am obsessed with details but having to execute all the details? I will struggle. That does not mean I

61

cannot (or will not) do it. But it does mean that I recognize where I should focus my attention. Understanding your strengths and blind spots will help you leverage your strengths and seek support for the areas that you might struggle with.

3. **Evaluate potential blind spots:** Sometimes, we are so focused on our goals that we miss potential pitfalls. This is where a critical evaluation comes in. I get teased by my partner for using business terms in our relationship (eek ... sorry, honey buns). It's where my brain naturally goes. I think in cognitive tools like SWOT (strengths, weaknesses, opportunities, threats) analysis to get a comprehensive view. It helps me to ask myself tough questions and be prepared for honest answers. What that does not help is the softer side of relationship skills necessary in a love relationship. So, I can also ask myself questions like "Am I being empathetic?" or "Am I communicating clearly and effectively" instead of using work tools to problem-solve? These are areas where my blind spots might lie, and by acknowledging them, I can work on improving them. By evaluating potential blind spots, we can prevent misunderstandings and conflicts in all aspects of our lives including our relationships.

Cognitive Tools for Decision-Making

Just like Dorothy's sharp wit and Rose's uncanny knack for storytelling, cognitive tools can help you navigate through decisions. These tools provide a structured way to evaluate your situation and make informed choices.

SWOT Analysis

This classic tool helps you assess your strengths, weaknesses, opportunities, and threats (SWOT). You can download lots of different

SWOT templates online and try this yourself. It's like having a heart-to-heart with Sophia Petrillo: brutally honest but ultimately helpful.

Personal example: When I was considering going back to school for my PhD, I did a SWOT analysis on myself. My strengths were my work ethic and experience, but my weaknesses were rusty research skills and limited free time as a single mom. The opportunity was advancing my career, but the threat was the cost and time commitment. In the end, I realized my strengths outweighed my weaknesses and the opportunity was worth the risk but the timing wasn't right.

Workplace example: Our team used a SWOT analysis when evaluating whether to launch a new suite of digital products. Our strengths were our brand reputation and loyal customer base. Weaknesses included limited production capacity and higher price point. The opportunities were entering a growing market and diversifying our offerings. Threats were strong established competitors and economic uncertainty. This honest assessment helped us plan strategically to capitalize on strengths and opportunities while mitigating weaknesses and threats.

I must admit, SWOT analysis only works if you are self-aware and self-reflective. I'm not sure about you, but for me, the one thing I really struggle with is being able to distinguish between opportunities and threats. Call it the way I grew up, where I grew up, the era I grew up in or just life, but fear of failure made nearly everything an opportunity, which kept me busy, scattered, and always chasing the next thing.

Decision Matrix

This tool helps you weigh each decision by assigning benefits and drawbacks and then assigning them a weight. It is great for making decisions when there are multiple options or factors to consider. You weigh the pros and cons of each choice and determine which one aligns best with your goals and values. You probably already have an informal decision matrix that runs through your mind but do not recognize it as that.

Personal example: When the queenager was choosing which college to attend, we used a decision matrix. Factors included academic programs, extracurriculars, location, and diversity. We rated each school on these criteria and gave them weighted scores based on importance. It helped us see objectively that the HBCU (historically Black college and university) she chose was the best fit, despite meaning out-of-state tuition and being far away from home base. The matrix took the emotion out of a tough choice.

Workplace example: My team used a decision matrix to select a new software vendor for our tech stack. Criteria included price, features, ease of use, and customer support. We scored each contender and the matrix clearly showed that although one option was cheapest, another provided the best overall value and user experience. Seeing it quantified on paper built consensus and confidence in our choice.

Cost-Benefit Analysis

Similar to the decision matrix, this tool helps you compare the costs and benefits of different choices. It also considers any potential risks or consequences that might come with each option. A warning: this is where many of us suffer from analysis paralysis.

Personal example: I did a cost-benefit analysis when considering whether to hire a housekeeper. On the one hand, it would free up time for family and self-care. But it also meant a financial cost and having a stranger in my home. Calculating the hours saved and assigning a dollar value helped me see that the benefits outweighed the costs. But I overthought it, calling references and debating the decision for weeks!

Workplace example: When our company was considering implementing a four-day work week, we analyzed the costs and benefits. Costs included potential client service gaps and reduced project hours. But benefits included improved employee morale, productivity, and retention. We even quantified the estimated savings in reduced turnover. The analysis showed it was worth a trial run, but it definitely sparked a lot of what-if spirals and number crunching along the way!

Eisenhower Matrix

This tool categorizes tasks based on their urgency and importance, helping you focus on what truly matters. You essentially categorize issues into urgent/nonurgent and important/unimportant boxes. Think of it as organizing your life with the efficiency of a TikTok home organizing video. Although we tend to behave in impulsive ways (why does watching an Instagram influencer unbox their Amazon packages make us feel like we have got to get every gadget right now?), this enables our brain to slow down to process what is needed at that moment.

Personal example: As a working mom, my to-do list is never-ending. Using an Eisenhower Matrix helps me prioritize. Urgent and important items like bill deadlines and things the queenager needs at school go in the "Do First" quadrant. Nonurgent but important things like exercise and friend dates are "Schedule." Urgent but less important things like returning an email go in "Delegate." And nonurgent, unimportant items like reorganizing the pantry get "Eliminated." It helps me focus my limited time and energy on what matters most.

Workplace example: As a CEO who is an active practitioner, every fire drill feels urgent. An Eisenhower Matrix helps me triage. True emergencies that affect business operations go in "Do First." Important but less time-sensitive work like long-term strategy goes in "Schedule." Busywork like expense reports are "Delegated." And distractions like office gossip are "Eliminated." Categorizing this way ensures the vital work gets prioritized amidst the daily chaos.

So, there you have it – a quick tour of cognitive tools to help you make better decisions at home and work. Whether you are choosing a school, software, or what to tackle on your to-do list, these frameworks can provide clarity and confidence. Just remember, even with these tools, decisions are rarely black and white. As my Mama Dawn would say, "You're damned if you do, and you are damned if you do not." But at least with these techniques, you can feel more like you are making an informed choice rather than a wild guess. And that, my friend, is half the battle!

Embracing Realistic Tactics

Creating a tactical plan grounded in reality is essential to avoid burnout. Ambition is great, but without a realistic plan, it can lead to overcommitment. And overcommitting leads to feelings of shame. And once shame sets in … sigh … well many of us quit. Here's how to keep it real:

- **Set clear priorities:** Identify what truly matters and focus on those areas. Where are my *A Different World* fans? Remember how Dwayne Wayne always prioritized his studies and relationship with Whitley? There could have been anything else going on but he was CLEAR. Be like Dwayne – know your priorities.

A Different World Primer

For those of you who have never seen *A Different World,* no worries. The show takes place in the 1980s at a fictional HBCU called Hillman College. It was a spin-off of *The Cosby Show.* The cast of characters includes students and locals, like the ever-quirky Dwayne Wayne, who is known for his iconic flip-up glasses and his relentless, often hilarious, attempts at romance. Dwayne starts off as a nerdy math whiz with a knack for getting into awkward situations, but over time, he evolves into a dedicated student, tutor, and

---

eventually a teacher. His on-again, off-again relationship with the Southern belle Whitley Gilbert keeps viewers on their toes, culminating in one of the most memorable TV weddings of the era.

- **Delegate and collaborate:** Do not try to do everything yourself. I am holding up the mirror to myself, too. I needed to learn that I am able to ask for support but I had to be clear about who I ask and be specific about what I am asking for. Being able to lean on one another, delegating tasks, and collaborating can lighten your load and bring in fresh perspectives.

- **Be flexible:** Life is unpredictable. I think sometimes we confuse change with volatility. Although they both relate to fluctuations, they are distinctly different. Change is about the overall movement of value, good or bad. Volatility is about risk no matter the direction. It activates our fight-or-flight instinct. When we feel like we are losing control, we are more likely to grasp for control. I always admired how Dwayne often had to adapt his plans, whether it was deciding to go to class or work or a sudden change in circumstances. Building flexibility into your plans to accommodate the unexpected means you leave space to change course.

Amelia's Story

Amelia stood by the window of her small but efficiently organized office, the morning sun casting long shadows across the desk cluttered with project files and budget sheets. She held a pen in one hand, tapping it idly against her chin as she gazed out at the bustling city street below. Her mind was a whirlpool of figures

(continued)

Check Up Before You Charge Up (reTHINK)

(continued)

and deadlines, swirling around the stark reality of her company's strained resources.

She had recently taken on a new project, lured by the potential prestige and profit it promised. Yet now, as she reviewed the numbers again, doubt crept in like an unwelcome shadow at dusk. *Had she overcommitted?* The question gnawed at her as she turned back to the spreadsheets.

The soft rustle of papers brought her attention to Tom, her assistant, who entered carrying more data for review. "Here's what you asked for," he said, placing a thick folder next to her on the desk. The thud it made seemed to echo her sinking heart.

"Thanks," Amelia replied absently, flipping through the top pages. Each page seemed to scream that what they had was not enough – neither time nor money nor people power seemed sufficient to meet the ambitious goals she needed to meet.

Tom watched her for a moment before speaking up hesitantly. "You know, maybe we need to reassess our capacity before taking another step forward." His voice was gentle yet firm, grounding yet somehow stirring a storm within Amelia.

She paused and looked at him sharply, surprised yet grateful for his frankness. *How often had she ignored such counsel in the past?* She pondered this as they both sat down to discuss their strategy once more.

As they talked through their options – scaling back some aspects of the project, seeking additional resources – Amelia felt a slow resurgence of control over her fears. It was not about admitting defeat but about steering toward success with prudence and foresight.

Outside, the city continued its relentless pace; people hurried along sidewalks under the bright glare of midday sun that streamed into Amelia's office now filling it with warm light that danced across their earnest faces.

As Amelia leaned back in her chair later that afternoon after Tom had left, still surrounded by papers but now with a clearer path forward etched out before them both mentally and on paper – a plan rooted in realism rather than wishful thinking – she mused silently: *Is our commitment to realism truly enough to safeguard against burnout?*

Real-World Application: Implementing Healthy Assessment in Your Organization

Integrating healthy assessment practices into your organization can lead to more sustainable success. Here are some steps to get started:

- **Establish a culture of assessment:** Encourage regular evaluations of resources at all levels of the organization. Make it a standard practice to assess before acting.

- **Use cognitive tools:** Implement tools like SWOT analysis and the Eisenhower Matrix to aid in decision-making. Upskill your team on how to use these tools effectively and adapt them to the intersectionality that is present in your organization.

- **Foster collaboration:** Promote a collaborative environment where team members can share resources and support each other. This can lead to more innovative solutions and efficient use of resources.

- **Embrace flexibility:** Be open to adjusting plans based on the outcomes of your assessments. Flexibility enables better adaptation to changing circumstances.

Conclusion: Advocating for Realistic Evaluation

As I wrap up this chapter, remember that a healthy assessment of your resources is not just a one-time task but an ongoing practice. By adopting these methodologies, you equip yourself with the knowledge to not just plan better but also achieve more with less – turning constraints into opportunities by listing all the resources you have available. This might include financial resources, human resources (such as colleagues or mentors), time, skills, equipment, and any other assets that could contribute to your success. **Being thorough in this assessment will give you a clear picture of what you have to work with and where there might be gaps that need to be filled.**

Once you have identified your resources, it's important to evaluate their capacity and limitations. Consider how much time you realistically have to dedicate to a project, the budget constraints you need to work within, and the expertise you can bring to the table. Understanding both the strengths and constraints of your available resources will help you set achievable goals and develop strategies that align with what is truly feasible.

Remember that being honest with yourself about your limitations is not a sign of weakness; rather, it is a sign of wisdom and self-awareness. **Acknowledging where you might need additional support or where you might be overextending yourself can prevent burnout and ensure that your efforts are focused on activities that will yield the greatest return on investment.** It's better to start small with manageable goals than to overcommit and risk falling short of your objectives.

By conducting a realistic assessment of your available resources, you are laying the groundwork for sustainable success. **This process enables you to make strategic decisions based on facts**

rather than wishful thinking, leading to more efficient use of your time and energy. Embrace this reality check as a tool for empowerment rather than a limitation because it equips you with the knowledge needed to navigate challenges effectively.

Just like the Golden Girls supported each other through thick and thin, be your own advocate. Assess, plan, and execute with a clear understanding of your resources and potential blind spots. This approach will help you achieve more with less stress and greater satisfaction.

So, grab a cup of iced tea, sit back, and channel your inner Golden Girl or Hillman alum. Remember, it's not about how busy you are, but how effectively you use your resources. You can make informed decisions, avoid burnout, and create strategies that lead to sustainable success. And always, always, keep a sense of humor along the way.

CHAPTER 5

THE PARADOX OF SELF-CARE SACRIFICE

WORKING SMARTER, NOT HARDER

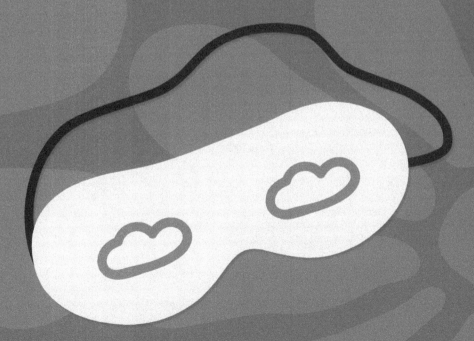

"I'm not bossy, I just have better ideas."

**MERYL STREEP AS MIRANDA PRIESTLY,
THE DEVIL WEARS PRADA**

Sure, Beyoncé has the same 24 hours in a day that you do, but let us be real – she's got an entire squad making her life run like clockwork. Without that same army, the key is to understand and activate how you can work smarter, not harder, and still rock your goals.

Manicures, Pedicures and Spa Days...Oh MY!

Friends! I am here to tell you that your health is all you got! That's it! That's the message. I struggled like hell in my 30s. Why? Because I was not dealing with my health. I did not think I had the time. I was unexpectedly divorced with a toddler. Every day felt like a remix of "Is THIS my life?" And "you have got to be kidding me!" I thought if I just paddled faster under water and worked harder that I would be able to regain my footing and get back on track. I also thought it would be really easy to remarry but that story is for another book. Teehee.

So, I worked and I worked and my parents helped me with the queenager and I worked. And I worked some more. I had a full-time job and built my company at night and on the weekends, I worked while she was in the pool at swim practice, and I sat on the bench. I worked while she was on the soccer field. I stayed up working for hours after she went to sleep, only to be up at 5:00 the next morning to begin my morning routine. Over and over. Year after year. And I tried to eat healthy and work out. That worked in cycles for years but eventually my "off" cycles became longer and longer. I developed sciatica, and I still did not stop or slow down working. I got a pinched nerve in my neck, and I did not stop working. I would have swollen hands from typing for so many hours a day, and I did not stop working. I developed high blood pressure and had to carry around a blood pressure machine when I was on the road, and ... yep ... I still did not stop working.

Here I was, a consultant, a business owner, and speaker talking about leadership and I WAS SICK Y'ALL. The reason I care so much about wellness and well-being and leadership is because I AM YOU. I know what it's like to just think "If I just work a little harder" knowing damn well that wasn't going to work. It wasn't until I could not walk for a week (Mama Dawn had to help me use the bathroom for days) that I said to myself, "Enough." I am not the only one who needed an *enough* moment. My client Emma did, too.

Emma's Story

The sun hung low in the sky, casting long shadows across the quiet suburban street. Emma walked home from the commuter train station, her mind a tangled web of thoughts. The crisp autumn air filled her lungs, and the rustle of leaves underfoot provided a rhythmic soundtrack to her contemplations. She had spent another 12-hour day at her desk, eyes glued to spreadsheets and emails, convinced that more hours would finally yield better results.

As she reached her front door, Emma fumbled for her keys. Her fingers trembled slightly from fatigue. She paused for a moment, looking at the key ring with its worn leather fob – a gift from her hubby years ago when she first started this job. It seemed like a lifetime ago when she believed in balance and self-care. Now, she was just trying to keep up with an ever-growing list of tasks.

Inside, the house was silent except for the faint hum of the refrigerator. She dropped her bag on the floor and headed straight for the bathroom. The mirror reflected dark circles under her eyes and a weariness that no amount of makeup could hide. As she got ready to take a shower, Emma thought back to a conversation with an old friend who had left corporate life for something simpler but more fulfilling.

"You're not Beyoncé," he had said with a chuckle over lunch one day. "You do not have an army of people making sure you can work those crazy hours."

Emma sighed deeply as got out of the shower. She knew he was right but felt trapped by expectations – both external and internal. Her mind wandered to an article she'd read about how self-care wasn't just about bubble baths or vacations; it was about daily practices that nurtured mental and physical well-being.

In the kitchen, Emma opened the fridge and pulled out some leftovers. Everyone was asleep so she tried to be as quiet as possible. As she heated them up in the microwave, she thought about reintegrating small acts of self-care into her routine – like taking short walks during lunch breaks or setting boundaries on work hours. She remembered how creativity used to flow effortlessly when she felt well rested and happy.

As she sat down at the dining table alone, fork in hand but appetite absent, Emma wondered if sacrificing herself on the altar of productivity was worth it anymore. Could embracing self-care truly lead to better outcomes in both personal and professional realms? And if so, why did it feel like such an impossible shift to make? The next morning, Emma found herself at the kitchen table, her eyes tracing the patterns on her ceramic mug. She decided to take a personal time off day. The steam from her lukewarm tea had long since ceased its dance into the air, and the quiet around her was almost palpable. She gazed out through the window where the sun cast a soft glow over dew-speckled grass. Even though she was supposed to be off, her email notifications kept singing their familiar ping, signaling another day that demanded more than she felt capable of giving.

The Paradox of Self-Care Sacrifice

Why Working Harder Is Not the Answer

More hours do not necessarily lead to better results. After years of coaching high performers who learned to prioritize self-care, I've noticed a common thread: they achieve great results without sacrificing their well-being. After nearly collapsing, one of my clients, Ayana, a powerful CEO with a high profile, transformed her approach to work after collapsing from exhaustion, focusing on finding more balance in her life and making time for her overall well-being. She learned the hard way so that you do not have to: self-care is not a luxury; it's essential for optimal performance. Numerous studies show how physical activity, proper nutrition, and adequate rest significantly improve cognitive functions such as memory, problem-solving, and creativity.

A healthy mind and body are foundational to sustained productivity and innovative thinking. Integrating self-care into daily routines does not have to be complicated or time-consuming. Simple practices like scheduling regular breaks, setting boundaries with work, and engaging in activities that bring joy can make a substantial difference. The key is consistency and recognizing the value these practices bring to overall well-being.

For too long, the prevailing belief has been that success is directly correlated with the number of hours we work. As illustrated by Emma, Ayanna, and me, that is a myth we are dismantling and replacing with a more sustainable approach: prioritizing self-care to enhance cognitive function. If you want to live a great life, you have got to slow down. I love my coffee but I cannot caffeinate myself to success. To be healthy and successful, you have got to be willing to redirect your energy. The bottom line is that you cannot be inspired if you are tired.

The modern workplace often glorifies busyness, but this mindset is detrimental in the long run. Shifting focus from quantity of work hours to quality of output can lead to more meaningful achievements. One of the key ingredients to being able to slow down and do less is to delegate. What Emma and I needed was a nitro shot of my Miami girls.

Delegation
Golden Girls Edition

Blanche's Approach to Delegation

Blanche Devereaux, with her endless charm, was a master at getting others to do her bidding. Whether it was talking Rose into baking a pie or convincing Dorothy to cover her shift at the museum, Blanche knew how to make delegation look easy. The key? Confidence and charm. When you believe in the importance of the task and approach it with a sense of grace, people are more likely to respond positively.

Dorothy's Directness

Dorothy Zbornak, however, took a more direct approach. She did not beat around the bush – she was clear and concise about what needed to be done and who needed to do it. This clarity is crucial in effective delegation. When you are clear about your expectations and the outcomes you desire, it leaves little room for miscommunication or half-hearted efforts.

Rose's Empathy

Rose Nylund might have been known for her St. Olaf stories, but she also had a unique way of empowering those around her with empathy and understanding. She knew that everyone had their strengths and weaknesses and played to those strengths. When delegating, it's essential to understand your team's abilities and

(continued)

The Paradox of Self-Care Sacrifice

(continued)

motivations. By doing so, you not only get the job done but also help your team grow and feel valued.

Sophia's Wisdom

Sophia Petrillo, with her sage advice and quick wit, taught us that sometimes the best way to empower someone is to share your wisdom and trust them to run with it. Delegation is not about micromanaging every step; it's about trusting others to use their skills and knowledge to achieve the desired outcome.

Now, imagine if Emma had the sass of Dorothy Zbornak, the wisdom of Sophia Petrillo, the charm of Blanche Devereaux, and the sweetness of Rose Nylund to guide her through the art of delegation. Maybe self-care wasn't just about taking a walk or eating better. Maybe, Emma needed to rethink her idea that *she* had to be the one that did everything.

This chapter is all about breaking down how to delegate gracefully, empower your support team, and use automation to master the regal art of having others do the work, so you can preside over your domain with ease. I also cover how you can kickstart your five-star wellness plan. But it starts with a healthy assessment of where you are *right now* before you decide to act.

Delegation and being healthy are more interconnected than you might think. By effectively delegating tasks, you can significantly improve your overall well-being.

Delegation comes much easier to me now. Why? Two things:

- I have a team I trust who will yank things off my plate.
- I trust myself to let go.

I could not figure out how some of my contemporaries were so good at delegating. They always seemed to have a "person" for things they needed done. I realized that all my years of over-functioning were creating the conditions for people around me – my team, my family, and my friends – to be under-functioners. I had to change by making myself *the* priority and creating my golden rules of delegation.

Kishshana's Golden Rules of Delegation

In the whirlwind of modern leadership, mastering the art of delegation is not just a skill – it's a necessity. Enter my golden rules of delegation, a transformative approach that turns the often-daunting task of sharing responsibilities into a powerful tool for team growth and organizational success.

This section delves into a set of principles designed to help leaders navigate the complexities of delegation with confidence and finesse. From understanding your own strengths to empowering your team members, these rules provide a road map for effective delegation that goes beyond simply assigning tasks. They offer a framework for building trust, fostering professional development, and ultimately creating a more dynamic and productive work environment. As you explore each rule, you'll discover how to leverage delegation not just as a means of managing workload, but as a strategic asset in cultivating high-performing teams and achieving your organization's goals.

Rule 1: Know Thyself and Thy Team

Dorothy Zbornak once said, "No one ever told me I was going to grow up to be a middle-aged woman." Well, no one ever told us that delegation would be the key to making it to and thriving during middle age either. The first step in delegation is understanding your

The Paradox of Self-Care Sacrifice

strengths and weaknesses, as well as those of your team. Why? When you know (and focus on) your strengths and learn to manage your weaknesses, you put yourself in a position to focus on what you are best in class at accomplishing.

- **Assess your team's strengths and weaknesses:** Understanding your team, their experience levels, and what they do best can help you determine which tasks to delegate and which to automate. For instance, if you have a detail-oriented wordsmith, delegate editing tasks to them. If you have a charismatic salesperson, let them handle client check-ins. When I stopped trying to improve my weaknesses and found a less soul-sucking way of managing them, life started looking up!
- **Match tasks to skills:** Just like Blanche would never let anyone else handle her social calendar, you need to ensure that tasks are matched to the right people. This not only ensures efficiency but also empowers your team members by playing to their strengths.

Rule 2: Communicate Clearly

Sophia Petrillo might have been known for her bluntness, but when it comes to delegation, clear communication is key. A lot of times your team, in the office and at home, are straight up confused when you are narrating what is needed. Mine must've been at times because they would smile and nod and then either not do what I delegated or come back with so many questions that I would end up doing it myself. I had to learn to do the following:

- **Clarify the tasks:** Clearly articulate the desired outcome. Begin with the end in mind and specify the desired results. If necessary, spell out the necessary steps and provide context for the task.

- **Set milestones and deadlines:** Outline the milestones or indicators used to track progress. This helps keep everyone on the same page and ensures that tasks are completed on time.

Rule 3: Let Go of Control

Blanche Devereaux once said, "I have a little rule about men: if they do not go away, I go away." The same can be applied to tasks. Once you delegate, let go of the control.

- **Avoid micromanaging:** Once you have given clear instructions, let your team members handle the task. Avoid micromanaging because it can interfere with their work process and undermine their authority.

- **Trust your team:** Trust that your team members will get the job done. This not only empowers them but also frees up your time to focus on more critical tasks.

- **Trust yourself:** If you were the hiring manager for your current team, trust that you hired the right people and let them go!

Empowering Your Support Team: Building a Culture of Open Communication

Rose Nylund might have been naive, but she always knew the importance of communication. Foster a culture of open communication within your teams and between your teams and leaders. This encourages clear feedback on the effectiveness of your processes and increases employee satisfaction.

And before you say, "Kish, I know all this," I'd bet my favorite pair of red bottoms that you aren't doing any of it. Culture at its most basic is a set of behaviors. When you are too busy, you are fostering a culture of anxiousness, overwhelm, lack of engagement, and, yes, burnout. Here are two things I've been able to maintain no matter how "busy" I am:

- **Regular assessments:** Conduct regular assessments of your team's workflows, ensuring tasks and processes are working as intended and providing a chance to identify any changes based on evolving needs or team members' strengths. This includes scheduled planning and debrief time for the various workstreams, annual retreats to recalibrate on the relationship norms for your team, and working sessions to sync on the work you are doing toward your goals.

- **Feedback loops:** Providing actionable feedback is critical to developing the professional skills of your team and also clarifies any expectations. Feedback works best when it's a two-way street. This means keeping a regular cadence of check-ins with each team member where you can be *fully present*. There is nothing worse than a team member coming into your office to talk with you and you spend 90% of your time looking at the screen or their having to repeatedly experience you canceling meetings (sometimes one minute before the start time!).

Training and Development

Listen, no matter how tough it was some days, I am grateful to my parents for the training and leadership development they provided for me. It made me both service-minded and tough as nails. Providing ongoing learning experiences in systems and skills ensures your team is equipped to handle delegated tasks and use technology tools and automation efficiently.

- **Invest in training:** Training takes time – so it's tempting to just do it yourself. But think of training as an investment in your team members and your own workload. Over time, you'll recoup the time you spent training because the person will be able to do work independently.

- **Embrace mentorships:** Delegating work might take a lot of time and mentorship, especially for the first few times or with new employees. However, it's a worthy investment. At the start, you might need to spend more time guiding them, but eventually, they will become self-sufficient. Time poor? I get it. The idea of spending more time when *you* need more time is frustrating as hell. And yet your ability to create spaciousness depends on it. But my Miami girls have taught us a thing or two about that already.

Once I have done a proper assessment of my people, I turn my attention to how to leverage technology to support them and, selfishly, get things off my desk so I can focus on what I really need to do. Y'all, I am nosy so a lot of times, I am in the mix with my team because I will not mind my business. Understanding *how* to use technology has helped me manage my time better and manage others with greater compassion.

Identifying Tasks for Automation

Automation and delegation aren't mutually exclusive. They can work together to help you optimize your workflow efficiency, especially when you find the right balance between the two.

- **Repetitive tasks:** Identify repetitive tasks that can be easily automated. This includes tasks like sending automated emails, scheduling social media posts, or generating reports. And now with so many tools supported by a growing web of AI applications, it is more possible to create a digital ecosystem that can remove the obstacle of repetitive tasks.

- **Complex tasks:** More complex or creative tasks require a more hands-on approach and are better suited for delegation rather than automation. To break tasks into subtasks effectively, follow these steps with real-life workplace examples:
  - Start with the end goal: For a marketing campaign, your end goal might be "Launch successful product X campaign."
  - Identify major components: Break this down into main tasks like "Develop marketing strategy," "Create content," and "Implement campaign."
  - Break down each component: For "Create content," subtasks could include these:
    - Write social media posts.
    - Design graphics for ads.
    - Produce promotional video.
    - Draft email newsletter.
    - Further divide if necessary: "Write social media posts" could be broken down into these subcategories:
      - Research trending hashtags.
      - Draft 10 Facebook posts.
      - Create 15 X posts.
      - Develop five LinkedIn articles.
- **Assign time frames:** Give each subtask a deadline, like "Draft 10 Facebook posts by Wednesday."
- **Prioritize:** Determine which subtasks are most critical or time-sensitive.
- **Allocate resources:** Decide who's responsible for each subtask or if it can be automated.

By breaking tasks down this way, you create a clear road map for your project, making it easier to delegate, automate, and track progress effectively.

Implementing Automation Tools

Listen, friend, I love my gadgets and have the Kickstarter receipts to prove it, but when it comes to automation, it's all about finding the right tools that fit your workflow.

- **Tailoring automation to fit your workflow:** Review automation solutions regularly to ensure the tools are working as intended or see if there are better solutions, especially because technology and products continue to evolve. Use tools like email filters, scheduling apps, and task management software to handle repetitive tasks. These not only save time but ensure consistency and accuracy. AI can help analyze data and provide insights, making it easier to make informed decisions quickly. Tools like predictive analytics can help forecast trends and identify opportunities, freeing you from the burden of data analysis.

- **Integrating your tools:** Ensure that your automation tools integrate seamlessly with your existing systems. This reduces the learning curve and makes the transition smoother for your team.

- **Outsourcing:** Sometimes, the best form of delegation (and automation) is outsourcing. Whether it's hiring a virtual assistant to manage your calendar or using a service to handle customer support, outsourcing enables you to focus on higher-level tasks.

Advocating for Realistic Evaluations: Taking an Honest Look at Your Resources

One thing I knew I could count on growing up was my parents ability to tell it like it is. They did not mince words, and they did not really try to spare my feelings when they needed to pivot and/or adjust. I'm not saying you need to be crass or rude (especially to yourself ... hello inner critic) but I do believe that it's essential to advocate for a realistic and honest evaluation of resources and potential impacts before implementing plans at work and at home.

- **Assessing situations accurately:** Use tools to assess situations accurately to make informed decisions. This includes evaluating the available resources, potential risks, and the expected outcomes.

- **Strategic planning:** Strategic planning involves setting realistic goals and timelines based on the available resources. This helps in avoiding overcommitment and ensures that the plans are achievable.

- **Starting a decision diet:** Take a pause so that you have the mental space to assess your current bandwidth and appetite for making this shift. This is probably the most impactful thing you can do to properly assess and prioritize your decisions. It's important to take breaks and step back from the constant flow of decision-making in order to make informed and well-thought-out choices.

Here's my take on a decision diet. I do not know about you but I am OVERWHELMED by the sheer number of decisions I need to make every day. I find myself struggling with what should be the simplest of tasks and I KNOW it's taking a toll on me. I first learned about decision diets in 2017. It was a particularly stressful year. I remember I was finally gaining some traction in my speaking career but it did not seem fast enough for me. I was struggling to keep up with my volunteer service commitments (and to be honest they were WEARING ME OUT), and my plate was in FULL effect as a mom. With swim meets, soccer tournaments, social activities for the kiddo, and trying to be out in the street, ya girl was tired. Brushing my teeth felt like a chore. Figuring out what to make for dinner became a 10-pound weight around my ankles. Getting dressed, something I actually LOVE, lost all its luster. I just wanted to s-t-o-p. My head hurt. My body hurt. My heart hurt. I needed a break. So I took a decision diet.

Interestingly, I had done this many times before, all the way back to my collegiate career. Just about every day for five years of my BS/ MBA program, I wore a uniform. Yep! I sure did. And not a ratty sweatshirt and pajamas (which to be clear, I would not be caught dead wearing). I wore a white t-shirt, blue jeans or a jeans skirt, a fly jacket, and dope shoes. DASSIT! I rarely deviated from that look and it was so freeing to not have to think about what I needed to wear, with a heavy course load, a full social calendar, leadership positions in school, and a whole long-distance relationship too! So in 2017, it wasn't a hard sell to take it back to basics. I started wearing a uniform again. I always wore the same brand of clothing when I traveled for work. Nordstrom got ALL my money. When I was home I wore the same brand of loungewear. Everyday. I ate the same type of food for months (thankfully, my mom cooked for my kiddo so she did not suffer while I did that). I took the same route on errands. I started waking up at the same time every day (which I still do to this day). Any decision that I could automate or put on cruise control I did. And the cloud started to lift.

Taking a decision diet from the things that keep you majoring in the minors is crucial. Focus on high-impact tasks and delegate or automate the rest.

The Paradox of Self-Care Sacrifice

- **Prioritize tasks:** Triage your to-do list by assigning tasks based on their urgency and importance. This helps in focusing on what truly matters and avoiding getting bogged down by minor tasks.

- **Set boundaries:** Establish clear boundaries between work and personal time. Learn to say no to tasks or commitments that do not align with your priorities or values.

- **Get into autopilot:** Choose to put decisions on cruise control for a while so that you can focus on the things that need the entirety of your executive functions.

Paralyzed by Purging: The Struggle with Letting Go

Just like Blanche struggled with letting go of her youth, many of us struggle with letting go of things that no longer serve us, whether it's clothing, food, or even old habits. So we do not start really assessing our time, talents, or our treasures because doing so means that we *might* have to confront the MESS we have created in our lives. Ouch! You are not alone in this. I've been telling you ALL my business, so let me share two things that I still struggle with from time to time:

- **Clothing:** I remember a time when I was paralyzed by the thought of purging my closet. Each piece of clothing held a memory, and letting go felt like losing a part of myself. But I realized that holding on to these items was only cluttering my space and my mind. It took releasing nearly 70 pounds and moving my whole life across the country to *finally* let go of the clothing I held hostage. I had to let go of parts of my past that held me hostage. Whew!

- **Food:** The same goes for food. I used to hoard snacks and treats, thinking I might need them someday. And I did not grow up food insecure either! But this only led to unhealthy eating habits and a cluttered pantry. Learning to let go and only keep what I truly needed was liberating. Now my pantry could be a star on TikTok!

Stories from Michelle Obama and Oprah Winfrey

Even Michelle Obama and Oprah Winfrey have their perspectives on delegation and letting go.

- Michelle Obama once shared how she learned to delegate tasks to her team to focus on what truly mattered. She emphasized the importance of trusting your team and letting go of the need to control everything. She once said, "We need to do a better job of putting ourselves higher on our own 'to-do' list." She emphasizes the importance of self-care and delegation in managing a busy life. By delegating tasks, you free up time to focus on what truly matters to you.

- Oprah Winfrey, however, has talked about the importance of purging not just physical items but also emotional baggage. She believes that letting go of what no longer serves you creates space for new opportunities and growth. Her advice? "You can have it all. Just not all at once." This means recognizing your limits and delegating effectively to maintain balance.

Conclusion

In a world that glorifies busyness and equates long hours with success, it's essential to challenge the notion that more time spent equals better results. The truth is, you are not Beyoncé. You cannot thrive

The Paradox of Self-Care Sacrifice

on endless work without taking care of yourself. Productivity is not about the quantity of hours you put in but the quality of work you produce. Constantly pushing yourself to the limit without allowing time for self-care can lead to burnout, decreased creativity, and overall diminished performance.

By embracing the principles of delegation, empowering your support team, and using automation, you can achieve more with less effort. Incorporating self-care practices into your daily routine is not a luxury but a necessity for maintaining peak performance and overall well-being. Remember, working smarter, not harder, is the key to sustainable success.

So, take a page from the Golden Girls and embrace the art of delegation. Empower your team, automate where possible, and prioritize your well-being. After all, life is too short to be busy all the time.

CHAPTER 6

THE ART OF THE ELEGANT BRUSH-OFF

(reTHINK): AN INCLUSIVE APPROACH TO SETTING AND REACHING GOALS

"I don't have any time to stay up all night worrying about what someone who doesn't love me has to say about me."

VIOLA DAVIS

Picture it: Miami, 1985. Four sassy seniors are gathered around a kitchen table, cheesecake in hand, dishing out wisdom like it's going out of style. Now, I might not be pushing 80 (yet), but honey, I've learned a thing or two about the fine art of saying no that would make Blanche Devereaux proud.

As a uni-mom, professional speaker, and recovering people pleaser, I've had more than my fair share of practice declining invitations, requests, and downright demands on my time and energy. And let me tell you, learning to say no with grace and conviction has been about as easy as convincing Dorothy to go on a blind date. But just like the Golden Girls, I've picked up some tricks along the way that I'm dying to share with you.

So grab a slice of cheesecake (or whatever treat floats your boat), pull up a chair, and let's dive into the delicate dance of setting boundaries, reaching goals, and embracing the power of no – all while keeping our Southern charm intact, of course.

The Sophia Petrillo School of Straight Talk

Now, I love Sophia's no-nonsense approach as much as the next gal, but let's face it – most of us can't get away with her level of brutal honesty without burning a few bridges. That said, there's something to be learned from her directness. When it comes to setting goals and managing our time, we could all use a little more of Sophia's clarity.

As a solo mom and oldest child, I spent years trying to be everything to everyone. Parent teacher association meetings, soccer practice, swim meets, you name it, I was there with bells on, even if I was secretly wishing I could be anywhere else. It was exhausting, and frankly, about as fulfilling as one of Rose's St. Olaf stories.

It wasn't until I channeled my inner Sophia and started being honest with myself (and others) about what I really wanted and needed that things began to change. I realized that saying yes to everything meant saying no to myself, my own goals, and the things that truly mattered to me.

So, here's your first lesson in the art of the elegant brush-off: be clear about your priorities. Write them down, say them out loud, tattoo them on your forehead if you have to (okay, maybe not that last one). But make sure you know what matters most to you, because that's the foundation for everything else.

The Blanche Devereaux Guide to Graceful Declination

Now, don't get me wrong – I'm not suggesting you start turning down every invitation and opportunity that comes your way. After all, life is meant to be lived, and sometimes the most unexpected experiences lead to the greatest joys. But there's a difference between being open to new possibilities and being a doormat.

This is where we can all take a page from Blanche's book. That woman knew how to decline an offer without ever making the other person feel rejected. It was all in the delivery, honey.

I remember one particularly grueling period when I was juggling my speaking career, single motherhood, and what felt like every volunteer position known to mankind. I was the team mom for both soccer and swimming, despite the fact that I couldn't tell a butterfly stroke from a backstroke and thought a hat trick was something you did with a fedora.

One day, as I was drowning in sign-up sheets and snack schedules, I had an epiphany. I didn't have to do it all, and more important, I didn't want to. It was time to channel my inner Blanche and start declining with the grace of a Southern belle dodging suitors at a debutante ball.

Here's how it went down: "Oh, sugar," I drawled (because in times of stress, my nonexistent Southern accent makes an appearance), "I'm just tickled pink that you thought of me to organize the end-of-season banquet. But you know, I've been spreading myself thinner than Blanche's negligees lately, and I'm afraid I just can't give it the attention it deserves. Why don't you ask Linda? She's got a real knack for these things, and I hear she makes a mean seven-layer dip."

And just like that, I was off the hook. No hurt feelings, no burnt bridges, just a graceful exit stage left.

The key to Blanche-style declination is threefold:

- Express appreciation for being considered.
- Offer a brief, honest explanation (without oversharing).
- Suggest an alternative if possible.

Practice this formula, and soon you'll be turning down requests with the finesse of a Southern debutante declining her third marriage proposal of the day.

Rose Nylund's Lessons in Setting Inclusive Goals

Now, I know what you're thinking. "Kishshana, what does our sweet, naive Rose have to teach us about setting goals?" Well, let me tell you, there's more to that St. Olaf farm girl than meets the eye.

Rose had a way of bringing people together, of seeing the best in everyone and including them in her plans. And when it comes to setting and reaching goals, both at work and at home, that inclusive approach can be a game changer.

In my years as a professional speaker and coach, I've seen countless organizations struggle with goal setting because they're not including all the right voices in the conversation. It's like trying to make a decision about what to watch on TV without consulting

Sophia – you're bound to miss out on some golden opportunities (and probably end up watching something terrible).

So, how do we channel our inner Rose and create a more inclusive approach to goal setting? Here are a few tips:

- **Cast a wide net:** Just like Rose would gather the whole town for one of her famous St. Olaf festivals, make sure you're including diverse perspectives when setting goals. This means reaching out beyond your immediate circle and actively seeking input from people with different backgrounds, experiences, and viewpoints.

- **Listen with an open mind:** Rose had a knack for hearing the wisdom in even the most outlandish St. Olaf tales. When gathering input for your goals, listen without judgment. Sometimes the best ideas come from unexpected places.

- **Find common ground:** Rose was a master at finding connections between people, no matter how different they seemed. When setting goals, look for shared values and aspirations that can unite your team or family.

- **Celebrate small wins:** Remember how excited Rose would get over the simplest things? Bring that enthusiasm to your goal-setting process by acknowledging and celebrating progress along the way.

- **Be willing to adapt:** Rose's stories often took unexpected turns, but she always rolled with the punches. Be flexible in your goal setting and willing to adjust course as needed.

By taking a more inclusive approach to setting and reaching goals, you're not only increasing your chances of success, you're also creating a more supportive and engaged community around you. And isn't that what we all want? A cheesecake-loving, problem-solving, ride-or-die squad like the Golden Girls?

Dorothy Zbornak's No-Nonsense Approach to Accountability

Alright, we've covered Sophia's straight talk, Blanche's graceful declination, and Rose's inclusive goal setting. But we can't forget about our dear Dorothy and her razor-sharp wit and unwavering standards.

Dorothy was the queen of holding people accountable – whether it was calling out Blanche's exaggerations, keeping Rose focused, or standing up to her mother's schemes. And when it comes to reaching our goals, we could all use a little more Dorothy in our lives.

As a recovering people pleaser, I used to struggle with holding myself and others accountable. I'd set goals, sure, but following through? That was about as likely as Sophia passing up the chance to make a sarcastic comment.

It wasn't until I embraced my inner Dorothy that things started to change. I realized that being kind doesn't mean being a pushover, and that holding people (including myself) accountable is actually an act of love and respect.

Here's how you can channel your inner Dorothy and boost your goal-reaching power:

- **Set clear expectations:** Dorothy never minced words. Be crystal clear about what you expect from yourself and others when it comes to your goals.

- **Follow up regularly:** Don't wait until the last minute to check on progress. Schedule regular check-ins, just like Dorothy would quiz her students.

- **Address issues promptly:** If something's not working, don't sweep it under the rug. Channel Dorothy's directness and address problems as soon as they arise.

- **Celebrate successes:** Dorothy might have been tough, but she was always quick to acknowledge achievements. Make sure you're recognizing progress and wins along the way.

- **Learn from setbacks:** When things don't go as planned, take a page from Dorothy's book and use it as a learning opportunity. Analyze what went wrong and how you can improve next time.

> **Note:** Remember, accountability isn't about punishment or criticism – it's about support and growth. By embracing Dorothy's no-nonsense approach, you're actually setting yourself and others up for success.

The Cheesecake Strategy: Finding Balance and Joy in What Matters

Now, I know we've covered a lot of ground here, and you might be feeling a little overwhelmed. But don't worry, honey – that's where the cheesecake comes in.

One of the things I love most about the Golden Girls is how they always came together at the end of the day, no matter what challenges they'd faced, to share a slice of cheesecake and some heartfelt conversation. It was their way of finding balance, reconnecting, and remembering what really mattered.

In our quest to set and reach goals, to say no to the things that don't serve us and yes to what truly matters, we can't forget the importance of joy, connection, and self-care. It's not about being busy for the sake of being busy – it's about creating a life that's rich, fulfilling, and sprinkled with plenty of cheesecake moments.

So, here's my proposal for what I like to call the "cheesecake strategy" for balanced goal setting:

- **Nourish your relationships:** Just like the Golden Girls always made time for each other, make sure your goals include nurturing your important relationships. After all, what's success without friends to share it with?

- **Indulge in self-care:** Treat yourself to regular moments of indulgence and self-care. It might not be cheesecake (or it might be – no judgment here) but find something that brings you joy and make it a non-negotiable part of your routine.

- **Laugh often:** The Golden Girls knew the healing power of a good laugh. Make sure your goals and your journey toward them include plenty of opportunities for humor and lightness.

- **Share your struggles:** Remember how the Golden Girls always turned to each other when times got tough? Don't be afraid to lean on your support system and share your challenges. You don't have to go it alone.

- **Celebrate the small stuff:** Every slice of cheesecake was an occasion for the Golden Girls. Find ways to celebrate your progress and small wins along the way to your bigger goals.

- **Stay flexible:** Sometimes the Golden Girls' plans went awry, but they always adapted. Be willing to adjust your goals and methods as life throws you curveballs.

- **Remember the big picture:** At the end of the day, the Golden Girls' friendship was what mattered most. Keep your core values and what's truly important to you at the center of your goal-setting process.

Putting It All Together: Your Golden Girls Guide to Goal Setting and Saying No

Alright, my darlings, we've covered a lot of ground here. We've learned how to channel Sophia's straight talk, Blanche's graceful declination, Rose's inclusive approach, and Dorothy's accountability. We've even sprinkled in some cheesecake wisdom for good measure. Now, let's put it all together into an actionable strategy for setting inclusive goals and mastering the art of the elegant brush-off.

- **Get clear on your priorities:** Channel your inner Sophia and get brutally honest with yourself about what really matters to you. Write it down, say it out loud, and make it real.

- **Set inclusive goals:** Take a page from Rose's book and involve diverse perspectives in your goal-setting process. Remember, the more voices you include, the richer and more robust your goals will be.

- **Learn to say no with grace:** Practice your Blanche-style declination. Remember: appreciate, explain briefly, and suggest an alternative if possible.

- **Hold yourself and others accountable:** Embrace your inner Dorothy and set clear expectations, follow up regularly, and address issues promptly.

- **Find your cheesecake:** Don't forget to build in moments of joy, connection, and self-care as you work toward your goals.

- **Stay flexible:** Life is unpredictable. Be willing to adapt your goals and methods as circumstances change.

- **Celebrate progress:** Take time to acknowledge and celebrate your wins, no matter how small.

- **Keep the big picture in mind:** Always remember your core values and what's truly important to you.

Now, I know this might seem like a lot to remember. But honey, if those four fabulous women could navigate the ups and downs of life in Miami with style and sass, you can certainly master the art of goal setting and saying no.

A Personal Note: My Journey from Yes Woman to Goal Getter

Before I wrap up this chapter, I want to share a bit more about my own journey from overwhelmed yes woman to empowered goal getter. As I mentioned, I spent years trying to be everything to everyone – the perfect mom, the star employee, the go-to volunteer. I was busier than Blanche at a firemen's convention, but I wasn't necessarily moving forward.

It wasn't until I hit a wall – literally and figuratively – that I realized something had to change. I was so exhausted from saying yes to everything that I actually walked into a wall at my daughter's school. There I was, sprawled out on the floor of the elementary school hallway, surrounded by parent teacher association flyers and sign-up sheets, wondering how on earth I'd gotten there.

That was my wake-up call. I realized that all my yeses were actually big nos to myself, my dreams, and my true priorities. I was so busy being busy that I'd lost sight of what I really wanted to achieve.

So, I started small. I said no to chaperoning the next field trip (channeling my inner Blanche, of course). I declined to bake cupcakes for the class party (with a gracious suggestion of store-bought alternatives). I even – gasp – stepped down from my position as team mom for both soccer and swimming.

And you know what? The world didn't end. The kids still had their field trip, the class still got their cupcakes, and the teams still had their snacks. But I had something I hadn't had in years – time and energy to focus on my own goals.

I started saying yes to speaking engagements that excited me. I carved out time to write the book I'd been dreaming about for years. I even started a global online community for Women of Color in Fundraising – something I never would have had the bandwidth for in my yes-to-everything days.

But here's the real kicker – by saying no to the things that weren't aligned with my true priorities, I actually became more present and engaged in the things I did say yes to. When I volunteered at my daughter's school, it was because I wanted to be there, not because I felt obligated. When I took on a new project at work, it was because I was genuinely excited about it, not because I was afraid to say no.

The journey wasn't easy. There were times when I felt guilty, times when I worried I was letting people down. But with each no, I grew stronger. I learned that setting boundaries and prioritizing my goals didn't make me selfish – it made me more effective, more fulfilled, and, honestly, a better mom, friend, and professional.

So, my dear readers, I challenge you to start your own journey. Channel your inner Golden Girl, embrace the power of no, and start setting goals that truly light you up. Remember, saying no to one thing is saying yes to something else – make sure that something else is worthy of your time and energy.

Conclusion: Golden Wisdom for a Balanced Life

As you come to the end of this chapter, I hope you're feeling inspired, empowered, and maybe even a little hungry for cheesecake. The wisdom of the Golden Girls might have come wrapped in laugh tracks and 1980s fashion, but it's just as relevant today.

Remember, busy isn't a badge of honor – it's often a four-letter word that keeps us from living our best lives. By embracing the art of the elegant brush-off, setting inclusive goals, and finding our own version of late-night cheesecake chats, we can create lives that are rich in meaning, purpose, and joy.

So the next time you're faced with a request that doesn't align with your goals, or you're setting objectives for your team or family, take a moment to ask yourself: what would Sophia, Blanche, Rose, or Dorothy do? Channel their sass, their wisdom, and their unwavering support.

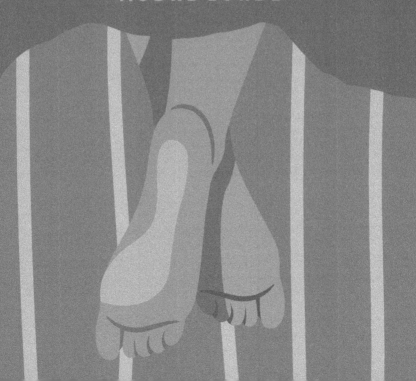

CHAPTER 7

SNOOZE MORE, SNORE LESS

REST IS NOT A

REWARD

THE CRITICAL ROLE OF DOWNTIME

"I have to remind myself that taking time for me is not selfish, it's necessary."

AUDRE LORDE

"I'm exhausted, girl. I feel like I've been running on empty for weeks," I sighed, collapsing onto the couch in my living room. My friend and sister Rochelle gave me a knowing glance.

"Honey, you are working yourself to the bone," Rochelle said, patting my hand. "Even I know when to take a break, and you know I work a lot, too!"

I laughed, grateful for my friend's support and wisdom. Her presence reminded me of lazy summer days spent with my brother and cousins in the hills of Spur Tree Hill, Jamaica, West Indies. The memory of red dirt beneath my feet and the scent of tropical flowers in the air made me long for simpler times. As I drifted off thinking about when I was going to book my next vacation, Rochelle's voice pulled me back to reality.

"You know, there's a *Golden Girls* episode that reminds me of your situation," Rochelle leans over and says to me while I sink deeply into my couch, my favorite beverage in hand. "Remember when Blanche hurt her back and the doctor ordered her to rest? She was going stir-crazy!"

I rolled my eyes. "Sis, that's not exactly helpful. I need to learn how to truly rest, not just lie in bed frustrated. I have done that enough already." Even though I burst out laughing at my own joke, I realized Rochelle was onto something. I worked seven days a week. If it wasn't client work, it was creating a new educational product. And when I wasn't working on something for my business I was doing something with my kiddo or my family or my sorority. I was always on the go. Looking back, I think I was afraid to slow down. I wasn't sure what would happen to me if I did. Like Blanche, I'd been viewing rest as a punishment rather than a necessity. It was time for a change in perspective before it was too late for me.

Snooze More, Snore Less: Rest Is Not a Reward

The Myth of Constant Productivity

For years, I'd bought into the myth that being constantly busy meant I was doing something. Friend, I felt important. I prided myself on my ability to juggle multiple projects, clients, and commitments. My calendar was a colorful mosaic of back-to-back meetings and deadlines. I wore my exhaustion like a trophy, convinced it was the price of success. Ohhh, friend, I was a workaholic who was quietly suffering from martyritis!

Martyritis: A chronic condition in which a person is unable to stop themselves from taking on roles and responsibilities that exhaust them and wildly inconvenience them but they want everyone to KNOW that they are suffering because they are important.

But as I sat there on the couch drifting between sleepiness and dreamland, I had to admit the truth: I was burning out. The constant hustle was taking its toll on my health, creativity, and relationships. I thought back to a quote from Jamaica Kincaid's *A Small Place* that had always resonated with me: "Every native would like to find a way out, every native would like a rest, every native would like a tour. But some natives – most natives in the world – cannot go anywhere."[1]

I had the privilege of choosing rest, yet I'd been denying myself that basic need. It was time to break free from the self-imposed prison of constant productivity. I am reminded of one of my favorite clients, Alex, and a story he told me about the morning he realized that he needed to rethink what it meant to be a top producer.

---

[1] Kinkaid, Jamaica. (2000). *A small place*. Farrar, Straus, and Giroux.

Alex's Story

The morning sun filtered through the half-drawn curtains, casting a warm glow on the cluttered desk in the corner of the room. Papers lay scattered, some crumpled, others covered in hastily scribbled notes. Alex sat hunched over, his fingers tapping rhythmically against the keyboard. His eyes darted between the screen and a notebook filled with ideas for his next project. He had been at it for hours, chasing a deadline that seemed to mock him with every passing minute.

His mind raced with thoughts of unfinished tasks and looming expectations. The weight of it all pressed down on him like an invisible hand squeezing his chest. He paused and rubbed his temples, trying to push away the fog of fatigue that clouded his thoughts. Memories of past nights spent in similar states of exhaustion flickered through his mind – nights where he had pushed himself to the brink, only to find that his creativity had dried up like a well in a drought.

A soft knock on the door pulled him from his reverie. Emily stepped into the room, her presence a gentle reminder that life existed beyond these four walls. She carried a tray with breakfast – toast, eggs, and fruit – setting it down beside him without a word. Alex looked up and met her eyes; they were filled with concern.

"Alex," she said softly, "you need to take a break."

He sighed heavily but nodded. He knew she was right; he could feel it in every ache and pain that throbbed through his body. Yet, there was an insistent voice inside him that whispered about deadlines and responsibilities, urging him to press on despite everything.

As he stood up and stretched, he felt a strange mix of guilt and relief wash over him. The room seemed brighter now as if acknowledging his decision to step back even for just a moment.

(continued)

Snooze More, Snore Less: Rest Is Not a Reward

(continued)

He walked over to the window and looked out at the garden below – a patchwork of vibrant greens dotted with bursts of color from blooming flowers.

The breeze carried the scent of jasmine through the open window, filling his lungs with its sweet fragrance. He closed his eyes and allowed himself to savor it for just a moment longer before turning back toward Emily.

"Maybe you are right," he admitted quietly.

She smiled warmly at him – a smile that held both understanding and encouragement – and took his hand in hers.

Together they walked into the living room where sunlight spilled across worn-out furniture creating patterns on faded upholstery; here was solace amidst chaos – a reminder that rest wasn't merely an indulgence but rather an essential part of their journey together.

In this brief pause from relentless striving came clarity: what if embracing rest could unlock new realms within their minds? What if allowing themselves moments away from work could lead them closer toward true fulfillment?

And so they sat side by side contemplating these questions while outside birds sang melodies, unburdened by deadlines or expectations, reminding them once more why integrating rest into their routine mattered not just today but always …

Why Waiting to Rest Is Costing You More Than You Think

This section dives into the real impact of always running at full throttle – on your mind and your body. Constantly pushing yourself to the max can lead to chronic stress, leaving you mentally drained and on the brink of burnout. Over time, this relentless pace can also take a toll on your physical health, causing everything from headaches and stomach issues to more serious problems like heart trouble. It's a gentle reminder that finding balance and taking care of yourself is not just nice – it's absolutely essential for staying happy and healthy in the long run.

The Body Keeps the Score

As I began to research the importance of rest, I came across Dr. Bessel van der Kolk's groundbreaking book, *The Body Keeps the Score*. His work on trauma and healing opened my eyes to the profound impact stress and burnout can have on our physical and mental well-being.

. One quote, in particular, stood out: "The greatest sources of our suffering are the lies we tell ourselves."[2]

I realized I'd been lying to myself about the sustainability of my frantic pace. My body had been sending signals – headaches, insomnia, irritability, high blood pressure – but I'd ignored them, pushing through with sheer willpower.

Dr. van der Kolk's research showed that chronic stress and trauma could literally rewire our brains and nervous systems. Without adequate rest and recovery, we become stuck in a state of hyperarousal, unable to fully relax or engage with the present moment.

This scientific perspective gave me a new appreciation for the wisdom of rest. It wasn't just about feeling refreshed; it was about allowing my body and mind to heal from the cumulative effects of stress. It hit me like a ton of bricks. I'd been chronically stressed out since my childhood. Marked as talented and gifted in the second grade, I spent years trying to live up to whatever that meant to my parents and to my teachers. I wasn't sure what I wanted to be when I grew up but I knew I wanted to be famous. But how? I was always on edge on the inside and bubbly bright and seemingly calm on the outside. I hid behind my

---

[2]van der Kolk, Bessel. (2015). *The body keeps the score: Brain, mind, and body in the healing of trauma* (p. 23). Penguin Books.

Snooze More, Snore Less: Rest Is Not a Reward

humor, my voice, and my big personality. No wonder I could not see the signs. I'd been lying to myself for a long time.

Creating My Five-Star Wellness Plan

As a Gallup CliftonStrengths Coach, I spend a lot of time working with leaders and their teams on how to leverage their strengths to meet and achieve outcomes *and* stay healthy and engaged at work. I talk about well-being and engagement a lot and take the time to help leaders reset their personal lives so that they can model healthier behaviors for their teams. I deeply believe that if you do not live well you cannot lead well. And I am not alone in my thinking. In 2010, Tom Rath and Jim Harter penned "The Five Essential Elements of Well-Being,"[3] an article that described the five elements of well-being that build resilient and thriving teams. I'd touched on this in my work for years but never sat down to think about how it applied to me (obnoxious, I know). Instinctively, I knew that a vision board with cute pictures of beautiful getaways and women in athleisure wasn't going to really contribute to my well-being; I would need to activate it. I wanted to have a tangible plan for my well-being that felt structured enough to replicate and flexible enough to adjust in each season of my life.

Pulling from the research Gallup has conducted, dozens of interviews with clients, hundreds of conversations with friends and family, and my lived experience, I developed what I call my "five-star wellness plan," a holistic approach to self-care and well-being that addresses five key areas of life:

- Physical wellness
- Emotional wellness

---

[3] Rath, T., & Harter, J. (2010, May 4). *Wellbeing: The five essential elements.* Gallup. https://www.gallup.com/workplace/237020/five-essential-elements .aspx

- Spiritual wellness

- Financial wellness

- Community wellness

Like the points of a star, these five areas are interconnected. When one is neglected, the others suffer. The key is finding balance, being able to integrate each part of your plan into the reality of your life, and adjusting your focus as needed throughout different seasons of your life.

Physical Wellness: Honoring Our Bodies

"The body keeps the score," Dr. van der Kolk reminds us. Our physical health is the foundation for everything else. Yet how often do we push our bodies to the limit, ignoring our limbs' pleas for rest?

I thought back to those carefree days in Jamaica, how my cousins and I would spend hours running through the hills, our bodies moving in perfect harmony with the natural world. There was no need to "exercise"; movement was simply a joyful part of life. My mind wandered to Double Dutch tournaments that lasted for hours as a kid and getting lost in Manhattan as a teenager walking for 50 city blocks before my legs started to hurt. When did it all change? After grad school? After giving birth? After I got divorced? I wasn't sure but I knew one thing. I needed a "Benjamin Button" moment. It was time to rethink … everything.

Now, as an adult, I had to be more intentional about caring for my body. I started small, by incorporating daily walks and stretching into my routine. Then I started going to Pilates, once a week and then three to four times. I started lifting weights and making better food choices. I paid attention to my sleep habits, creating a relaxing bedtime ritual free from screens and work-related stress.

As Rose would say, "Back in St. Olaf, we had a saying: "A body at rest stays at rest, but a body in motion falls down a lot." Although her folksy wisdom might be questionable, the importance of balancing activity and rest is undeniable. I used to resent people who rested. It felt to me like they were not "doing anything." Eventually, I realized that what I resented was my inability to choose myself. To choose rest.

> *"We become what we do – even when those things are outside of who we want to be. Our bodies are our teachers and the messengers who call our attention to what we are absorbing and becoming. This is why we have to learn how to listen, and this is why grounded confidence requires embodiment."*
>
> – Brené Brown

Emotional Wellness: Embracing Our Feelings

In our culture of toxic positivity, it's easy to fall into the trap of suppressing "negative" emotions. *Toxic positivity* is an excessive and ineffective overgeneralization of a happy, optimistic state that minimizes and dismisses negative emotions, experiences, or situations. It is the belief that people should maintain a positive mindset regardless of how difficult or challenging their circumstances are. It involves dismissing or avoiding negative emotions and experiences in favor of a forced positive outlook. There's an overwhelming pressure to maintain a cheerful facade at all times, even in the face of genuine hardship or distress. This obsession with "good vibes only" and the constant push to "be nice" can lead to the suppression of authentic emotions and experiences. Although positivity can be beneficial, its toxic counterpart often invalidates people's struggles, creating an environment where individuals feel compelled to mask their true feelings behind a veneer of forced optimism.

This societal expectation to always be positive can be particularly harmful in situations where acknowledging and processing negative emotions is crucial for mental health and personal growth. It can lead to emotional avoidance, when people deny or minimize their own or others' pain, potentially exacerbating psychological distress in the long run. Moreover, this culture of relentless positivity can create a sense of shame or inadequacy in those who cannot maintain the expected level of cheerfulness, further isolating individuals during challenging times.

As Dr. van der Kolk's research shows, emotions are the body's way of processing experiences and information. Ignoring them only leads to greater stress and disconnection. I started focusing on emotions more because I realized that I was an adolescent, emotionally. Focusing on my emotions was something I felt like I did not have time to do. I had a kid to raise and a business to grow. I was in survival mode. I really did not know where to begin so I went back to the basics.

I started incorporating mindfulness practices into my daily routine, taking time to check in with my feelings without judgment. Sometimes this meant sitting with discomfort or acknowledging difficult emotions I'd been avoiding. Years before, I'd stumbled onto an emotions researcher, Brené Brown, and instead of just using her quotes in my presentations, I grabbed a highlighter and started studying. By the time her *Atlas of the Heart* was published by Random House in 2021, I was ready to activate my growing lexicon for emotions. Friend, aren't emotions complex? No wonder many of us focus on the "mad, sad, glad" trio.

I started incorporating deliberate periods of "doing nothing" into my routine. Sometimes this meant taking a leisurely walk without my phone, other times it was simply sitting in silence for a few minutes. To my surprise, these moments of apparent "unproductivity" often led to my most creative breakthroughs. I stopped listening to music that did not lift my spirit. I scrubbed my social media pages so that it wasn't filled with what I thought were reminders that I had not arrived. And, I took my ass to therapy. I realized I was angry. No. I had RAGE from what seemed like a lifetime of settling for what I received instead of going after what I wanted. I'd been burying myself in my work and my life as a mom and could not afford to deal with the range of emotions that I experienced daily. But it was killing me. And I had to ask myself, what kind of example was I setting for my child? I did not want her to grow up thinking that she needed to work herself beyond exhaustion and suppress the fullness of her emotions in order to be successful. I had to break free of the binds of being an emotional runner.

Spiritual Wellness: Connecting to Something Greater

Spirituality does not have to mean organized religion (though it can). For me, it's about cultivating a sense of meaning and purpose beyond the day-to-day grind. It's tapping into that childlike wonder I felt exploring the lush Jamaican countryside. It's about my relationship with my Creator. I realized that I was on autopilot spiritually, which left me empty, dragging, and using all my "light" just to get through the day.

First, I kickstarted a deeper prayer life and started incorporating moments of stillness and reflection into my routine. Sometimes this meant formal meditation, other times it was simply pausing to appreciate the beauty of nature or express gratitude for the good things in my life. Then I started journaling. Not every day, but often enough to track my moods and any patterns that I had to reteach myself to recognize. I elevated my morning routine to become my morning ritual.

You might be wondering what I mean. At its root, the difference between a routine and a ritual is the mindset behind the action. So, I had to shift my mindset. My daily routines felt like actions that I needed to check off my to-do list. As I moved from routines to rituals, I noticed that having a meaningful practice for how I started and ended my day felt purposeful. It was like I got off autopilot. Once I made that shift, I saw an immediate increase in my joy and my productivity.

Financial Wellness: Creating Stability and Freedom

Money stress can be a major barrier to rest and well-being. Although financial wellness looks different for everyone, the key is finding a balance between security and flexibility.

I took a hard look at my spending habits and financial goals. I'd been working since I was 14 and loved working. My money story meant that I treated money like it was going to run away and I needed to spend it before it did. And I deeply believed there would be more to make. But where did the money actually go? When I wasn't doing well financially, it showed in how I treated myself in every other aspect of my life. Was I working so hard because I truly needed to, or was I caught in a cycle of lifestyle inflation? Ugh, I had to work that out in therapy. I also created a spending plan that allowed for both saving and occasional indulgences. Is it perfect? No. Am I perfect? Aht Aht! But I kept putting one foot in front of the other.

As Blanche would say, "I've always depended on the kindness of strangers ... but a healthy retirement account does not hurt either!"

Community Wellness: Nurturing Connections

Humans are social creatures. Even the most introverted among us need meaningful connections to thrive. Yet in our busy lives, relationships are often the first thing we neglect. Think about the number of times you skipped a get-together or event you really wanted to attend because of something work related. Maybe you actually make it to the event but you are distracted because your Slack keeps pinging and your phone keeps buzzing. Between showing up for the queenager at all her activities and my growing business, it felt like I never had time for myself let alone anyone else. I realized I was missing out on the precious moments when magic happens: in my relationships.

I made a conscious effort to prioritize quality time with friends and family. This meant saying no to some work commitments to make space for game nights, heart-to-heart conversations, and simply being present with loved ones. I made less money and missed some opportunities to grow my company and my personal brand. I even lost a helluva lot of footing as the social sector Black "It" girl because I did not want to be everywhere all the time at the expense of my family and my health. But let me tell you something, friend. I would do it again without a second thought. There is no amount of money or notoriety worth the memories I created with my kiddo, my mama, my brother, and my besties.

Community is like the pit stop in a NASCAR race. Even if you pull in for four minutes, you have everything you need to keep lapping this track called life.

Seasons of Life and Shifting Priorities

One of the most important lessons I've learned is that wellness is not a static state. Our needs and priorities shift as we move through different seasons of life. What worked for me in my 20s might not serve me in my 40s. The key is to regularly check in with yourself and adjust your five-star wellness plan accordingly. I find when I am focused on my wellness plan, I am able to rest. I am able to pause and slow down, and the restlessness that lives in me chills out. I needed a plan for rest. You might be able to get to your own personal slowdown differently. But if you are not able to ... give my five-star wellness plan a try.

I thought back to Jamaica Kincaid's words about the complexity of time and memory: "The past is a room full of baggage and rubbish and sometimes things that are of use, but if they are of real use, I have kept them."[4]

This applies to wellness practices as well. We must be willing to let go of habits or beliefs that no longer serve us, while holding onto the wisdom we have gained along the way.

Rest as a Radical Act

In a world that glorifies busyness, choosing to prioritize rest can feel like a radical act. It requires us to challenge deeply ingrained beliefs about productivity and self-worth. But as Dr. van der Kolk's research shows, rest is not just a luxury – it's essential for our physical and mental health.

Moreover, rest plays a vital role in stress reduction. Chronic stress can have detrimental effects on both our physical and mental health. Incorporating moments of rest and relaxation into our daily lives can help mitigate the harmful impact of stress, leading to improved overall well-being. When we prioritize rest as an essential part of our routine, we are better equipped to handle the challenges that come our way with resilience and clarity.

By making rest a non-negotiable part of maintaining productivity, we create space for creativity to flourish. Rest enables our minds to wander, make connections, and generate innovative ideas. When we are constantly in motion without giving ourselves time to pause and reflect, we limit our capacity for creative thinking. Recognizing the necessity of integrating rest into our routines opens up opportunities for inspiration and breakthroughs in our work and personal projects.

I'm reminded of another powerful quote from *The Body Keeps the Score*: "Being able to feel safe with other people is probably the

---

[4] Kinkaid, *A small place.*

Snooze More, Snore Less: Rest Is Not a Reward

single most important aspect of mental health; safe connections are fundamental to meaningful and satisfying lives."[5]

Creating space for rest enables us to cultivate those safe connections – with ourselves, with others, and with the world around us. It's in those moments of stillness that we often find our greatest insights and most profound healing.

The Creativity Connection

As a writer and creative professional, I've always prided myself on my ability to generate new ideas. But I'd fallen into the trap of believing that creativity required constant output. In reality, some of my best ideas came during moments of rest and reflection. Rest is a powerhouse for creativity. When your mind is free from constant work-related stress, it has the freedom to wander and explore new ideas. This unstructured time allows for better problem-solving and innovative thinking. Research supports that activities like daydreaming or engaging in hobbies unrelated to work can lead to creative breakthroughs. By scheduling regular downtime, you create the mental space needed for these moments of insight.

I thought back to those summers in Jamaica, how the simple act of cloud watching or listening to the rhythm of crickets at night would spark my imagination. I'd lost touch with that effortless creativity in my pursuit of productivity.

Tip: Embrace the idea that rest is not a luxury but a fundamental component of achieving your full potential. Remember, it's in moments of stillness that we often find our greatest insights and most profound healing.

---

[5] van der Kolk, *The body keeps the score*, p. 23.

Let us delve deeper into how rest affects creativity and stress reduction and explore practices that ensure rest becomes an integral part of your daily life.

Rest is not just a luxury; it is a necessity for maintaining productivity and well-being. **Taking breaks and allowing your mind to rest can have a profound impact on your creativity and stress levels.** Research has shown that when we give ourselves the time to relax and unwind, our brains are better equipped to generate new ideas and think outside the box.

Dr. van der Kolk's research supports the idea that rest is essential for creative thinking. When we are constantly in fight-or-flight mode, our brains do not have the capacity for the kind of divergent thinking that leads to innovation. And my career depends on my ability to be innovative and think outside the box.

As Sophia might say, "Picture it: the summer of 1666. A young Isaac Newton takes a nap under an apple tree. He wakes up with the idea for the theory of gravity … and a bruise from a falling apple. The point is, sometimes you gotta let your brain marinate!"

The Ripple Effect of Rest

As I began to prioritize rest and implement my five-star wellness plan, I noticed something unexpected: my productivity actually improved. I was able to accomplish more in less time because I was working from a place of energy and clarity rather than exhaustion.

But the benefits extended far beyond my to-do list. My relationships deepened as I had more emotional capacity to truly listen and engage. My creativity flourished, leading to exciting new projects and opportunities. Most important, I felt a sense of peace and contentment that had been missing for far too long.

- **The impact of rest goes beyond just feeling refreshed; it directly influences our cognitive abilities.** We know that adequate rest can improve memory consolidation, enhance decision-making skills, and boost overall cognitive function. By making rest a non-negotiable part of our routines, we set ourselves up for success in both our personal and professional lives.

- Furthermore, **restorative practices such as mindfulness and meditation have been proven to reduce anxiety and improve emotional well-being.** By engaging in these activities regularly, you can cultivate a sense of calm and clarity that enables you to navigate challenges with greater ease. Prioritizing rest is not a sign of weakness but rather a strategic choice to optimize your mental health and performance.

- Incorporating intentional rest breaks throughout the day can lead to increased productivity and efficiency in the long run. **By taking short breaks to recharge, you can avoid the pitfalls of decision fatigue and maintain focus on your tasks.** These moments of respite serve as opportunities to reset your mental state and approach your work with renewed energy and clarity.

- Remember that rest is not a reward for working hard; it is an essential component of sustainable productivity. **By recognizing the positive impacts of rest on creativity and stress reduction**, you can proactively design your daily routine to include moments of relaxation and rejuvenation. Embrace rest as a powerful tool for enhancing your well-being and achieving long-term success in all areas of your life.

Adopting Practices for Non-negotiable Rest

To ensure rest becomes an integral part of maintaining productivity, it's essential to adopt specific practices that prioritize downtime. Start by setting clear boundaries between work and personal time. This might mean turning off work notifications after a certain hour or designating specific times for breaks during the day. Another effective strategy is to incorporate micro-breaks – short intervals of rest in your working hours – to keep energy levels consistent.

> **Practical Examples:** Consider real-world examples when structured rest leads to success. Tech companies like Google have nap pods for employees to take short rests during their workday because they understand the boost in productivity that follows a brief period of relaxation. Similarly, many creative professionals schedule "think weeks" when they step away from their usual tasks to recharge mentally and explore new ideas without distractions.

Innovative Approaches in Leadership

Forward-thinking leaders are already embracing these concepts by promoting work cultures that value balance over busyness. They encourage flexible schedules, offer mental health days, and provide resources for stress management – all aimed at fostering an environment where employees feel valued and perform at their best. But this is all performative if it does not extend to your life outside of work.

- Incorporating practices that prioritize rest as a non-negotiable part of your routine is essential for maintaining productivity and overall well-being. **By adopting strategies that ensure rest is a fundamental component of your daily life, you can experience increased creativity, reduced stress levels, and enhanced effectiveness in both work and personal endeavors.** One effective way I made rest a priority was to schedule it into my day just like any other important task. By treating rest time with the same level of importance as meetings or deadlines, I signaled to myself and others that it is a vital aspect of my routine.

- **Create boundaries around your rest time by setting clear expectations with colleagues, friends, and family members.** Communicate openly about the importance of your downtime and establish guidelines for when you will be unavailable for work-related matters. By establishing these boundaries, you reinforce the value of rest in your life and create a supportive environment that respects your need for relaxation and rejuvenation.

- **Implementing rituals that signal the transition from work to rest can help you unwind effectively.** Whether it's a short walk outside, listening to calming music, or practicing deep breathing exercises, these rituals can cue your mind and body that it's time to shift gears and relax. Consistency in these rituals can also train your brain to associate them with relaxation, making it easier to unwind and recharge during your designated rest periods.

- **Consider incorporating mindfulness practices into your daily routine to enhance the quality of your rest time.** Engaging in activities such as meditation, yoga, or journaling can help quiet the mind, reduce stress levels, and promote a sense of inner peace. By cultivating mindfulness, you can deepen your connection to the present moment, enabling yourself to fully relax and recharge during moments of rest.

- **Prioritize self-care activities that nourish both your body and mind.** This could include getting regular exercise, eating nutritious meals, getting enough sleep, and engaging in hobbies or activities that bring you joy. Taking care of yourself holistically can have a profound impact on your overall well-being and energy levels, making it easier to stay productive and focused when you return to work.

- **Experiment with different forms of rest to discover what works best for you.** Although some individuals might find solace in solitude and quiet reflection, others might thrive in social settings or through engaging in creative pursuits. By exploring various forms of rest – from physical relaxation to mental stimulation – you can identify the practices that resonate most with you and incorporate them into your routine consistently.

- **Ultimately, by making rest a non-negotiable part of maintaining productivity, you not only enhance your own well-being but also set a positive example for those around you.** Embracing a culture that values rest as essential to success can lead to healthier work environments, increased creativity, and improved overall performance. By prioritizing rest alongside productivity, you create a sustainable foundation for long-term success and fulfillment in both your professional life and personal life.

Recognizing the Importance of Rest

I realized that by taking care of myself, I was better equipped to care for others and have a positive impact in the world. It was like the safety instructions on an airplane: I needed to secure my own oxygen mask before assisting others.

I realized that I wasn't resting just for myself. I'm resting for all the women who came before me who never had the chance to put their feet up.

Creating Your Own Five-Star Wellness Plan

Now it's your turn. I invite you to take some time to reflect on your own well-being and create a personalized five-star wellness plan. Remember, this is not about perfection or following someone else's rules. It's about tuning into your own needs and honoring them. Here are some questions to consider for each point of the star.

Physical Wellness

- How does your body feel right now?
- What kind of movement brings you joy?
- Are you getting enough quality sleep?
- How can you nourish your body with food that makes you feel good?

Emotional Wellness

- What emotions have you been avoiding or suppressing?
- How can you create space to process your feelings in a healthy way?
- What self-care practices help you feel grounded and centered?

Spiritual Wellness

- What gives your life meaning and purpose?
- How can you incorporate moments of stillness or reflection into your day?
- What practices help you feel connected to something greater than yourself?

Financial Wellness

- What is your current relationship with money?
- Are your spending habits aligned with your values and long-term goals?

- How can you create more financial stability and freedom in your life?

Community Wellness

- Who are the people who support and uplift you?
- How can you nurture those relationships?
- Are there new connections you'd like to make or communities you'd like to join?

Remember, your five-star wellness plan is a living document and practice. It should evolve as you move through different seasons of life. The key is to check in with yourself regularly and make adjustments as needed.

"A plan is just a dream with a deadline. 'So dream big, but be flexible!'"

– Rose, *The Golden Girls*

Embracing the Journey

As I wrap up this chapter, I'm reminded of another powerful quote from Jamaica Kincaid: "And so you needn't let that slightly funny feeling you have from time to time about exploitation, oppression, domination develop into full-fledged unease, discomfort; you could ruin your holiday."[6]

Although Kincaid was speaking about the complexities of tourism and colonialism, her words resonate with our journey toward rest and well-being. It's easy to ignore the "slightly funny feeling" that

---

[6] Kinkaid, *A small place.*

something is not right in our lives. We push down our discomfort, convincing ourselves that addressing it would be too disruptive.

But true rest and wellness require us to lean into that discomfort. We must be willing to examine our habits, beliefs, and choices with honesty and compassion. It's not always easy, but the rewards are immeasurable.

As you embark on this journey of rest and self-discovery, try channeling the spirit of the Golden Girls. May you approach life with Dorothy's wit, Blanche's confidence, Rose's optimism, and Sophia's irreverent wisdom. May you find the courage to prioritize your well-being, even when the world tells you to keep pushing.

And, most important, may you remember that rest is not a reward for productivity; it's an essential ingredient for a life well lived.

CHAPTER 8

FLEXIBILITY IN THE FACE OF RESISTANCE

NAVIGATING SHIFTS IN CULTURE AND VALUES (reTHINK)

"I've learned that you can't have everything and do everything at the same time."

OPRAH WINFREY

Culture and values are fundamental to how you live your life or lead an organization. As your organization grows, you might experience shifts in culture and values that need navigating. reTHINK culture means staying in tune with the changing needs of your team and being proactive in addressing them.

Let me tell you, friend, *busy* might be a four-letter word, but so is *shift* – and I'm not talking about the kind Dorothy Zbornak pulled at the local high school as a night school teacher. I'm talking about those seismic changes that rock the very foundation of your organization faster than Blanche Devereaux could say "Hey, y'all!"

As leaders, we are often so caught up in the day-to-day hustle that we forget to take a step back and really examine the culture we are cultivating. We're like Rose Nylund, plowing ahead with our St. Olaf stories without realizing our audience has long since tuned out. But here's the thing: culture and values are the bedrock of any organization. They're what separate the Hillman Colleges from the Hudson Universities, if you catch my drift.

Now, I know what you are thinking. "Kishshana, I've got deadlines to meet, quotas to hit, and a stack of paperwork higher than Whitley Gilbert's hair. Who has time to worry about culture?" Well, let me tell you something, friend – if you do not make time for culture, culture will make time for you. And trust me, you do not want to be caught off guard when that shift hits the fan.

The Golden Rule of Cultural Shifts

In one episode of *The Golden Girls,* the ladies decide to start a sandwich shop. They had the best intentions, but before long, they were at each other's throats faster than you could say "Picture it: Sicily." Why? Because they did not take the time to align their values and expectations.

The same thing happens in organizations all the time. We get so caught up in growth and expansion that we forget to check if everyone's still on the same page. Before you know it, you have got a culture clash bigger than the one between Dwayne Wayne and Ron Johnson in their early Hillman days.

> **Note:** Never saw *A Different World?* Flip back to Chapter 4, where you can find a quick synopsis of this ground-breaking show.

So, what's a leader to do? Well, for starters, we need to reTHINK our approach to culture. And no, I do not mean in the way 1990's fashion keeps swinging back in style (hello, I am so ready to let go of my asymmetrical bangs). I'm talking about a genuine, deep dive into the values that drive your organization and the people in it.

As a solo mom and oldest child, I've had my fair share of moments where I felt like my life gaps were holding me back. But let me tell you something – it took some real growth to understand those gaps aren't negatives. They're the spaces where growth happens. They're the moments that shape us, challenge us, and ultimately make us stronger leaders.

For the entirety of my career, I was the only Black woman – and almost always the only chief executive of color – on the leadership team. It was lonely and toxic and damaging to my psyche, and everyday felt like I was taking the long walk to the gauntlet. I would wake up with what felt like heartburn every day. I mean I was barely sleeping and yet I felt like no matter how hard I paddled under water I wasn't going anywhere. This was NOT what I expected to experience when I started my career. Talk about a "different world," right? It felt like I was constantly code-switching between Queens girl Kishshana and bland but palatable Kishshana, trying to find my place in a culture that wasn't always designed with me in mind.

But here's the thing – those experiences, as uncomfortable as they were, taught me invaluable lessons about navigating cultural shifts. They showed me firsthand the importance of creating inclusive cultures where everyone feels valued and heard. Because let us face it, I had enough experience being an outsider with my face pressed up against the glass of an exclusive club I only got an occasional visitor pass to, and it's not a pleasant feeling.

As I continued to navigate my career, I carried these lessons with me and used them to build inclusive teams and workplaces. I made sure to create spaces where everyone felt welcome and their voices were heard, regardless of their background or identity.

But it wasn't always easy. There were times when I faced resistance from colleagues who did not understand the importance of diversity and inclusion, equity and belonging. And there were moments when I doubted whether my efforts were making a difference.

That's where the power of co-conspirators comes in. Throughout my career, I have been fortunate enough to have co-conspirators – people who might not have shared my experiences but recognized the value in promoting diversity and inclusivity. They stood by me, supported me, and helped me push for change.

Co-conspirators are not just allies; they are active participants in the fight for equity and justice. They listen and educate themselves on issues affecting marginalized communities. They use their privilege to amplify marginalized voices and advocate for diversity and inclusion in all aspects of life.

From Pet to Threat: The Black Woman's Tightrope

Now, let us talk about a phenomenon that's all too familiar to Black women in professional spaces – going from pet to threat. It's a journey more treacherous than Sophia's trip from Sicily to Brooklyn, and twice as exhausting.

Close your eyes and walk with me. You start a new job and everyone's falling over themselves to tell you how "articulate" you are, how "refreshing" your perspective is. You're the flavor of the month, the golden child, the pet project. Some executive even has the audacity to say they will "mentor" you but makes no efforts to do anything but set you up for failure and wonder why you failed. But then something shifts. Maybe you start speaking up more in meetings, challenging the status quo. Suddenly, those same people who were singing your praises are looking at you like you are a threat to their very existence. You have team members sneaking off to HR to complain about your "tone" but never addressing it with you. You are walking in a professional minefield blind, hoping you do not step on a career-crippling grenade.

It's a dance as delicate as trying to guess Cyndi Lauper's age! One misstep, and you are labeled as "aggressive" or "difficult." But take it from me, friend – better to be a threat than a pet any day of the week.

Navigating this transition requires a level of emotional intelligence that would make even Michelle Obama or Ted Lasso proud. You've got to be aware of the shifting dynamics, adapt your approach without compromising your integrity, and find folks who see your value beyond tokenism.

It's not easy, but remember – Oprah did not become the strong, confident woman we all know and love overnight. It took time, growth, and a whole lot of believing in herself. So channel your inner Oprah, hold your head high, and show them what you are made of!

Leading with Flexibility: The Dwayne Wayne Approach

Now, let us talk about leading with flexibility. And no, I do not mean doing the splits like Blanche at a dance audition. I'm talking about the kind of adaptability that would make Dwayne Wayne and his flip-up glasses proud.

In *A Different World*, Dwayne starts off as this goofy, lovesick puppy chasing after Denise. But as the series progresses, we see him grow into a strong, principled leader. He learns to adapt his approach without compromising his values, whether he's dealing with the antics of Ron and Walter or the challenges of dating Whitley.

That's the kind of flexibility we need as leaders navigating cultural shifts. We need to be able to bend without breaking, to adapt our style without losing sight of our core principles.

Navigational flexibility is pivotal in steering an organization through the complexities of change. It involves adaptive decision-making processes that allow for adjustments in strategy without derailing the overall objectives. This approach enables leaders to remain responsive to feedback and evolving circumstances, thereby reducing friction and enhancing the likelihood of successful outcomes.

I remember a time when I was leading a major organizational change. The resistance was thicker than Whitley's deep Southern drawl. I knew I had to find a way to get buy-in without steamrolling over people's concerns.

So, I channeled my inner Dwayne Wayne. I listened. I adapted. I found ways to incorporate people's feedback into the change process. And you know what? It worked. We were able to navigate the shift without losing the essence of our organizational culture.

Note: Flexibility is not about being a pushover. It's about having the emotional intelligence to read the room, the wisdom to know when to stand firm and when to compromise, and the courage to admit when you need to change course.

Flexibility in the Face of Resistance (reTHINK)

Navigating the turbulent waters of organizational change is a formidable task for any leader. Resistance is a natural response, yet it is often the most significant barrier to implementing necessary shifts within an organization. The challenges are manifold, stemming from deeply ingrained habits to fear of the unknown. Part of being able to achieve more by doing less is understanding these challenges, equipping leaders around you with strategies to overcome them through navigational flexibility, and ensuring that core values are upheld amidst transformation.

Understanding Resistance: The Sophia Petrillo Guide

When it comes to understanding resistance, we could all take a page out of Sophia Petrillo's book. That tiny Sicilian spitfire could read people better than Blanche could read a room full of eligible bachelors.

Resistance to change is as natural as Rose reaching for another slice of cheesecake. It's human nature to cling to the familiar, even when we know change is necessary. As leaders, our job is not to eliminate resistance – it's to understand it, work with it, and ultimately, channel it into positive energy for change.

I've found that resistance often comes from a place of fear. Fear of the unknown, fear of failure, fear of losing status or control. It's like when Dorothy was resistant to Sophia dating – it wasn't really about the dating, it was about her fear of losing her mother.

So, how do we address this resistance? Well, for starters, we need to create safe spaces for people to express their concerns. And I do not mean the kind of "safe space" where you lure a team member into a false sense of security and then pull a switcheroo and penalize them for being honest. I'm talking about fostering an environment where people feel heard and valued, even when they are expressing doubts or concerns. It's about acknowledging the validity of their feelings while also helping them see the bigger picture.

I remember one particularly challenging culture shift when I was met with fierce resistance from a long-time employee. I inherited this person when I started, and she got results but her social skills left a lot to be desired. I knew that it could not be all work and perhaps something else was happening. Instead of dismissing her concerns or trying to steamroll over them, I took the time to really listen. I channeled my inner Sophia, cutting through the BS to get to the heart of the matter.

Turns out, her resistance wasn't about the change itself; it was about feeling like her years of experience and expertise were being overlooked. Folded into that was her children had recently moved back home, and they treated her home like a hotel and not the home they grew up in. Work was the place she felt in control, and these changes were rocking her locus of control. Once we addressed that underlying concern, she became one of the biggest champions for the change.

Resistance in organizational settings typically manifests as a reluctance or outright refusal to accept changes. This stems from various factors, including fear, misunderstanding, and a perceived threat to personal or group interests. Leaders must first identify and understand these underlying causes of resistance to address them effectively. By acknowledging and empathetically engaging with these concerns, leaders can begin to dismantle barriers, paving the way for meaningful dialogue and eventual acceptance of change.

Strategies for Overcoming Resistance and Fostering Organizational Resilience

Navigational flexibility is a crucial skill for leaders when guiding teams through organizational change. It involves the ability to pivot, adapt, and steer the team in the right direction despite facing resistance. Flexibility enables leaders to adjust their strategies, communication methods, and approaches based on the feedback and challenges encountered during the change process.

Active Listening and Open Communication

One key aspect of navigational flexibility is active listening. Leaders must be attuned to the concerns, fears, and feedback from team members as they navigate cultural changes. By listening actively, leaders can address issues promptly, demonstrate empathy, and build trust within the team. This fosters a sense of collaboration and inclusivity, essential for successful change implementation.

Openness to Feedback and Adaptability

Another vital component of navigational flexibility is being open to feedback. Leaders who are willing to accept input from their team members can gain valuable insights into the impact of cultural changes on different individuals or departments. This openness creates a culture of transparency and encourages team members to share their thoughts and concerns openly.

Adaptability is a core skill within navigational flexibility. Leaders must be prepared to modify their plans, timelines, and approaches based on evolving circumstances or unexpected challenges. By staying agile and adaptable, leaders can respond effectively to resistance and keep the change process on track.

Empowering Team Members

Navigational flexibility also involves empowering team members. Leaders should delegate tasks, encourage autonomy, and provide support to team members during cultural changes. Empowered employees are more likely to embrace change, take ownership of their roles, and contribute positively to the transformation process.

Conflict Resolution Skills

Conflict resolution skills are essential within navigational flexibility. When faced with resistance or disagreements during cultural changes, leaders must be able to manage conflicts constructively. By addressing conflicts promptly and effectively, leaders can prevent disruptions, maintain morale, and keep the change initiative moving forward smoothly.

Celebrating Small Wins

Celebrating small wins is another key aspect of navigational flexibility. Recognizing and rewarding progress, no matter how small, can boost morale, motivation, and engagement within the team. This positive reinforcement reinforces the benefits of change and encourages continued participation from team members.

Maintaining Core Values While Embracing Change

Navigating through organizational changes while upholding core values is a delicate balance that requires strategic finesse. Maintaining the foundational principles of an organization while embracing necessary adaptations is crucial for sustained success. Leaders must cultivate an environment where evolution is not seen as a threat to tradition but as a means of growth and relevance in a rapidly changing world.

Embracing change does not mean abandoning what makes an organization unique; rather, it involves aligning the core values with the evolving needs of the market and stakeholders. Adapting with integrity requires thoughtful consideration of how each modification aligns with the organization's mission, vision, and ethical standards.

In the process of organizational transformation, leaders must be vigilant in preserving the essence of their organization's identity. This entails communicating transparently with all stakeholders to ensure that changes are understood within the context of the organization's overarching purpose and values. By fostering open dialogue and feedback mechanisms, leaders can instill confidence in their team members that the changes are not eroding the foundation but strengthening it for future challenges.

Leadership that endures is built on a solid foundation of unwavering values coupled with a dynamic approach to change. Organizations that successfully navigate cultural shifts while staying true to their core principles are those that prioritize authenticity and consistency in their actions. By demonstrating a commitment to both tradition and innovation, leaders can inspire trust and loyalty among their team members, fostering a culture of adaptability and resilience.

Adaptive Leadership: Lessons from Hillman College

If there's one thing *A Different World* taught me, it's that leadership is not a one-size-fits-all proposition. I did not just learn that tuning into a new episode every week. I also saw this at home, where my dad showed leadership very differently than my stepdad, and my mom had everyone under her thumb, but you'd never know.

Adaptive leadership is about recognizing that different situations call for different approaches. It's about being able to read the room – whether at work or home – and adjust your style accordingly. Think about Whitley's journey throughout the series on *A Different World*. She starts off as this pampered Southern belle who cannot seem to do a thing for herself, but by the end, she's a strong, capable woman who can hold her own in any situation. That's adaptive leadership in action.

As leaders navigating cultural shifts, we need to adapt our approach based on the needs of our team and the demands of the situation. Sometimes, you need to be firm and directive, like Colonel Taylor dealing with a campus crisis. Other times, you need to be more nurturing and supportive, like Dean Hughes mentoring a struggling student.

I've found that the key to adaptive leadership is self-awareness. You need to understand your own strengths, weaknesses, and biases. You need to recognize when your default leadership style is not working, and you need to have the flexibility to try something new. It's like that time I was leading a cross-functional team on a high-stakes project. My usual collaborative, consensus-building approach wasn't cutting it. The team was stuck in endless debates, and we were falling behind schedule. I realized I needed to channel my inner Colonel Taylor. I stepped up, made some tough decisions, and got the team moving again. Was it comfortable? About as comfortable as Dwayne Wayne in a suit and tie. But it was what the situation called for, and it got us back on track.

Managing Intergenerational Teams: Navigating Busyness and Work Perspectives

Navigating change with intergenerational teams at work and raising young people two generations younger than me has been a fascinating journey. It's like living in two different worlds simultaneously, each with its unique challenges and opportunities.

Pros and Cons of Intergenerational Teams

Working with intergenerational teams can be both rewarding and challenging. On the one hand, it drives innovation. Younger team members who have grown up during the Digital Revolution bring fresh perspectives and are more open to embracing new technology. On the other hand, mature professionals contribute their specialist knowledge and industry experience, guiding younger colleagues to achieve practical business objectives.

However, different working styles and communication preferences can lead to misunderstandings. For example, baby boomers and Gen Xers might prefer face-to-face communication, and millennials and Gen Zers are more comfortable with digital media and social platforms. This diversity requires a higher level of awareness and adaptability from leaders to ensure effective collaboration.

I turned to the internet to find practical examples of intergenerational conflicts from pop culture. Here are some movies and TV shows that come to mind:

- *Hacks* (2021): This show highlights the generational clash between Deborah Vance, an aging comedian, and Ava, a young comedy writer. Their relationship evolves from conflict to mutual respect, showcasing the potential for intergenerational collaboration.

- *Only Murders in the Building* (2021): This series brings together different generations through a shared interest in true crime podcasts, illustrating how common goals can bridge generational gaps.

- *The Chair* (2021): Set in a college, this show explores the tensions and collaborations between older professors and younger faculty members, emphasizing the importance of adapting to new ideas while respecting traditional values.

Raising Young People Two Generations Younger

Raising a young person who is two generations younger than me has been quite the adventure. The gap between the 1980s and 1990s versus now in 2024 is immense. Back then, we planned our Friday nights around the TGIF lineup, setting the VCR to record our favorite shows if we were not going to be home. Today, young people have everything on demand, streaming their favorite shows and movies whenever they want.

This generational gap presents challenges and opportunities. On the one hand, it can be difficult to relate to their experiences and the pressures they face, such as the constant connectivity and the impact of social media on their mental health. On the other hand, it offers a chance to learn from each other. For instance, while I might share stories about the simplicity and charm of shows like *Empty Nest* or *Full House*, the queenager can introduce me to the latest trends on TikTok or the newest music genres blending old and new influences.

Adaptive Leadership in Intergenerational Teams

Adaptive leadership in intergenerational teams and raising young people requires a blend of insight, empathy, and flexibility. By embracing these differences and learning from each other, we can navigate the complexities of change and build a more inclusive and innovative future.

Consider these strategies for managing intergenerational teams (also known as "you cannot do everything yourself; please let these professionals learn how to activate their education"):

- **Establish trust and respect:** Build mutual trust through regular check-ins and open communication.

- **Encourage knowledge sharing:** Create mentorship programs and collaborative projects to facilitate learning across generations.

- **Normalize employee feedback:** Implement regular feedback mechanisms to ensure all voices are heard.

- **Set clear expectations:** Clearly define goals and expectations to align team efforts.

- **Educate the team:** Promote the benefits of a multigenerational workforce through training and awareness programs.

- **Use employee coaching:** Offer coaching to help employees develop skills and grow professionally.

By implementing these strategies, leaders can harness the strengths of a diverse workforce, fostering a culture of collaboration and innovation that benefits everyone involved.

Preserving Core Values Amidst Change

A critical aspect of implementing change without losing sight of an organization's identity is maintaining its core values. These values serve as a compass that guides decision-making and actions throughout the transformation process. Leaders must ensure that every change initiative aligns with these values, reinforcing the organization's culture and strengthening trust among stakeholders.

Leadership in this new era demands more than just directive authority; it requires a blend of insight, empathy, and adaptability. The ability to not only anticipate resistance but also effectively manage it through flexible leadership practices is essential for any leader looking to foster an environment that embraces change while maintaining its foundational principles.

Anticipating and Addressing Common Challenges

When implementing cultural changes within your organization, it is essential to anticipate and understand the common challenges and resistance that might arise. Resistance to change is a natural response from individuals who are comfortable with the status quo. It can stem from fear of the unknown, lack of understanding about the reasons for change, or concerns about how the changes will affect their roles or the organization as a whole. Leaders must be prepared to address these challenges head-on to successfully navigate through the process of cultural transformation.

One of the key challenges faced when implementing cultural changes is employee resistance. Employees who have been accustomed to working in a certain way might feel threatened by new initiatives that disrupt their routines or challenge their established norms. This resistance can manifest in various forms, such as skepticism, reluctance to participate, or outright opposition. Leaders need to proactively engage with employees, communicate openly and transparently about the reasons for change, and involve them in the decision-making process to mitigate resistance effectively.

Lack of alignment within the organization is another common hurdle that leaders encounter when driving cultural change. Different departments or teams might have conflicting priorities, goals, or values, leading to internal friction and hindering cohesive progress toward the desired cultural shift. It is crucial for leaders to foster alignment by clearly articulating the vision for change, establishing common goals that resonate with all stakeholders, and creating a shared sense of purpose that unites the organization toward a common objective.

Moreover, institutional inertia can pose a significant barrier to cultural transformation. Organizations that have been operating in a certain way for an extended period might be resistant to change due to entrenched systems, processes, or beliefs that uphold the existing culture. Overcoming institutional inertia requires leaders to challenge outdated practices, drive innovation, and create an environment that encourages experimentation and continuous improvement. By breaking free from traditional mindsets and embracing adaptability, organizations can overcome inertia and pave the way for lasting change.

In addition to internal challenges, external factors such as market dynamics, regulatory changes, or technological advancements can also affect cultural transformation efforts. As a leader, you must stay attuned to external forces that might influence your organization's

Flexibility in the Face of Resistance (reTHINK)

culture and be prepared to pivot strategically in response to changing circumstances. By remaining agile and proactive in your approach, leaders can navigate external challenges effectively while staying true to their vision for cultural change.

Emotional Intelligence: The Glue That Holds It All Together

Now, let us talk about emotional intelligence. And, no, I do not mean the kind of intelligence that lets you come up with St. Olaf stories on the fly (sorry, Rose). I'm talking about the ability to recognize, understand, and manage your own emotions, as well as the emotions of others.

In the world of *The Golden Girls*, Dorothy was the queen of emotional intelligence. She could cut through the drama with a witty one-liner, but she also knew when to offer a shoulder to cry on or a word of encouragement.

As leaders navigating cultural shifts, emotional intelligence is our secret weapon. It's what enables us to read the room, to sense the undercurrents of resistance or enthusiasm, and to respond in a way that moves the organization forward.

I remember a particularly tense meeting where emotions were running higher than Blanche's libido. People were talking over each other, tempers were flaring, and we were getting nowhere fast.

That's when I channeled my inner Dorothy. I took a deep breath, called for a time-out, and addressed the emotional elephant in the room. I acknowledged people's fears and frustrations, validated their feelings, and then refocused the conversation on our shared goals and values.

It wasn't easy. It felt about as comfortable as a young person learning to walk in heels or a young person learning to shave. But by addressing the emotional aspect of the situation, we were able to move past the conflict and find a way forward.

Embracing Diversity: More Than Just a Hillman Motto

One of the things I loved about *A Different World* was how it showcased the diversity within the Black higher education community. From Whitley's Southern belle to Dwayne's Brooklyn swagger, from Kim's driven premed student to Ron's laid-back musician, the show demonstrated that there's no one way to be Black.

As leaders, we need to embrace this kind of diversity in our organizations. And I'm not just talking about racial diversity (although that's certainly important). I'm talking about diversity of thought, experience, background, and perspective. I'm talking about the visible AND invisible intersectionality's present in the workplace.

Let us face it: navigating cultural shifts without diversity is like trying to sail a ship with one oar. You just end up going in circles. But when you embrace diversity, it becomes your secret weapon. Different perspectives? They're not just nice to have – they are essential. They help you spot those pesky blind spots, conjure up innovative solutions, and build a culture that's genuinely inclusive. Do not believe me? Let us dive into the evidence.

First up, Ely and Thomas (2001)[1] did some heavy lifting to show that diverse teams aren't just a corporate buzzword – they are a powerhouse. Their research reveals that when you mix different perspectives in a team, you get better group processes and individual experiences. Translation: diversity helps you see what you are missing and come up with brilliant ideas.

---

[1] Ely, Robin J., & Thomas, David A. (2001). Cultural diversity at work: The effects of diversity perspectives on work group processes and outcome. *Administrative Science Quarterly, 46*(2), 229–273.

And if that's not enough to convince you, the folks at Great Place to Work® (2020)[2] have some juicy insights, too. They found that diverse and inclusive teams are the new engines of innovation. Imagine that – a team that actually values input from everyone, leading to groundbreaking ideas and a culture that's not just inclusive in name but in practice.

So, next time someone tells you diversity is just a checkbox, hit them with the facts. Diversity is not just our greatest asset in navigating cultural shifts – it's the only way to do it right.

I've seen firsthand the power of embracing diversity during times of cultural shift. In one organization, we were struggling to adapt to a rapidly changing market. Our traditional approaches were not working, and morale was lower than the chances of the Dallas Cowboys winning the Superbowl. (Ouch … yeah, I said it!)

That's when we decided to shake things up. We created diverse, cross-functional teams and gave them the freedom to experiment with new approaches. The results were amazing. By bringing together different perspectives and experiences, we were able to generate innovative solutions that none of us could have come up with on our own.

The Power of Authenticity: Keeping It Real in a Fake World

If there's one thing both *The Golden Girls* and *A Different World* teach, it's the power of authenticity. Whether it was Sophia's brutal honesty or Freddie's unapologetic activism, these shows celebrated characters who stayed true to themselves. The seed of being "myself" was planted by my dad before I can even remember, who always told me that I am my only competition.

---

[2] Great Place to Work. (2024). Why diverse and inclusive teams are the new engines of innovation. Great Place to Work (blog), July 25.

As leaders, authenticity is our superpower. In a world of corporate doublespeak and PR spin, people are hungry for leaders who tell it like it is. Telling it like it is does not mean being mean or cruel. It means being able to hold honesty and transparency while making space for differing opinions, ideas, and decisions. When we are navigating cultural shifts, this authenticity can be the difference between success and failure.

Note: Being authentic does not mean being perfect. It means being real, being vulnerable, and being willing to admit when you do not have all the answers. It's about leading with your values and your heart, not just your head.

I remember a time in the early years of my career when I was struggling with a major organizational change. The pressure was intense, and I felt like I was supposed to have all the answers. But the truth was, I was scared and uncertain. And if I am being honest, my mind wasn't on the current situation at work. I was worried about needing to move out of my apartment and how that would affect my kiddo's school. I had to shake that off and refocus and really draw on my faith and my upbringing to make a decision about how things were going to go.

That's when I decided to take a page out of Mama Dawn's book and just tell the truth. My mom is known to say, "I do not mean to hurt your feelings. I'm calling this how I see it." In a company-wide meeting, I admitted that I did not have all the answers. I shared my fears and my hopes. And you know what? Instead of losing respect, I gained it. People appreciated my honesty and were more willing to join me on the journey.

Allison's Story

The sun was already high, casting a sharp glare off the glass buildings of downtown when Allison stepped out of the revolving doors of her office building. The city buzzed around her; cars honked and pedestrians chatted on their phones or to each other, all moving with a purpose that she found both comforting and isolating. Her mind, however, was locked in a fierce internal debate over the cultural changes she was tasked with implementing at her firm.

As she walked toward the park for her usual lunch escape, Allison could feel the weight of resistance from her team. It clung to her like the city smog – thick and unrelenting. They had voiced their concerns loudly in meetings; changes were unsettling, they argued, possibly even unnecessary. Allison understood their fears; after all, she too had felt the sting of uncertainty when upper management laid out their new vision – one that promised innovation but demanded transformation.

Sitting on a sun-warmed bench beneath an old oak tree, whose leaves whispered in the gentle breeze, Allison watched a young mother trying to corral her energetic toddler. The child laughed gleefully as he dodged her outstretched arms, completely absorbed in his game. She smiled faintly. The scene mirrored her own challenges – guiding a team that did not always want to follow.

She remembered reading about navigational flexibility – the ability to steer through change while maintaining stability – and wondered how she could apply this concept more effectively. Could she become more adaptable in guiding her team through these turbulent times while still holding onto the core values that defined the corporate identity?

A squirrel scurried past her feet, startling her out of her reverie and reminding her that life continued unabated despite one's internal crises. She thought about how trees bend flexibly in strong winds yet rarely break. There was a lesson there about resilience and adaptation that resonated with Allison deeply.

As she tossed crumbs from her sandwich to some eager pigeons pecking near her feet, Allison considered how overcoming resistance within an organization required understanding it first – not just pushing against it blindly. Maybe what they needed was more open dialogue; perhaps if everyone felt heard and involved in shaping the change, resistance would turn into cooperation.

The clock tower nearby chimed one o'clock – a reminder that time moved forward relentlessly. Allison needed to head back soon but lingered for a moment longer in the quiet park, pondering how best to lead her team through this transition without losing sight of who they were as a company.

The Cheesecake Solution: Finding Common Ground

Now, I cannot talk about *The Golden Girls* without mentioning cheesecake. That delicious dessert was more than just a late-night snack – it was a symbol of friendship, comfort, and problem-solving.

In our organizations, we need to find our own "cheesecake moments" – times when we can come together, let our guards down, and really connect as human beings. These moments are crucial when we are navigating cultural shifts. They help build trust, foster understanding, and create a sense of shared purpose.

I've found that some of the most important conversations happen in these informal settings. It's amazing what can be accomplished over a shared meal or a cup of coffee. These are the times when barriers break down, when people feel comfortable sharing their real thoughts and feelings. If your organization is too big or too fractured, this will not work for you. Making a commitment to retreats (real ones not just long meetings with food) and step-backs (opportunities to pause and interrogate what is happening in the organization) are other ways I have learned to do this and, in the process, make my load as a leader a lot lighter.

So, like Allison, as you are navigating your own cultural shifts, do not forget to create space for these "cheesecake moments." They might just be the key to bringing your team together and moving forward as one.

Conclusion: Embracing the Journey

As I wrap up this chapter, I want you to remember something: navigating cultural shifts is not about reaching a destination. It's about embracing the journey.

Like the ladies of *The Golden Girls* or the students of Hillman College, we are all on a journey of growth and change. There will be challenges along the way. There will be moments of doubt and fear. There will be times when you feel like throwing in the towel and moving to Sicily (or St. Olaf, if you are feeling particularly masochistic).

But here's the thing – those challenges are what make the journey worthwhile. They're what help us grow, as individuals and as organizations. They're what push us to be better, to do better, to create cultures that truly reflect our values and empower our people.

So, embrace the journey, my friends. Channel your inner Dorothy when you need wisdom, your inner Blanche when you need confidence, your inner Rose when you need optimism, and your inner Sophia when you need to tell it like it is.

Remember, culture is not something that happens to us – it's something we create together, every single day. So let us create cultures that are as vibrant, diverse, and resilient as the casts of our favorite shows.

And if all else fails, well … there's always cheesecake.

CHAPTER 9

REVOLUTIONIZING REST:
THE UNSEEN
POWER⚡HOUSE
OF PRODUCTIVITY

KNOW WHEN TO REST BEFORE YOU ACT
(reTHINK)

"Dear sleep, I'm sorry we broke up this morning. I want you back!"

ANONYMOUS

In an era when burnout has become a badge of honor and continuous hustle is glorified, the need to shift organizational culture toward embracing rest is not just beneficial – it's imperative. Remember the movie *Hitch*? Will Smith plays a dating consultant who advises Kevin James's character, Albert, to take a step back and "just breathe" before making his next move. It's a lesson in pacing – knowing when to act and when to rest. Just as Albert's dating success depended on his ability to balance his enthusiasm with patience, so too does the success of modern organizations hinge on their ability to integrate rest as a fundamental component of their operations.

The landscape of leadership is undergoing a profound transformation, one where sustainable performance and well-being are at the forefront. This evolution requires us to rethink traditional work paradigms and integrate rest as a core component of organizational health. The foundation of this transformative approach lies in normalizing rest within the workplace. By fostering an environment where taking breaks is viewed as essential rather than optional, organizations can unlock a host of benefits that go beyond mere productivity. It's about creating a workspace where employees are not just allowed but encouraged to recharge, leading to enhanced creativity, improved decision-making capabilities, and a more engaged workforce.

But as I sit here, sipping my coffee and staring at my overflowing calendar, I can't help but chuckle at the irony. Here I am, Kishshana Palmer, supposed productivity guru, feeling like I'm drowning in a sea of commitments. It's like that classic scene from *The Golden Girls* where Dorothy says, "I'm exhausted just looking at you." Well, honey, I'm exhausted just looking at my own schedule!

Growing up, I was taught that idle hands were the devil's playground. My mama would often say, "Kishshana, if you're not busy, you're not living!" So, I filled every waking moment with activities, clubs, and responsibilities. I was the queen of multitasking, the empress of overcommitment. I thought I was living my best life, but in reality, I was just running myself ragged.

As the oldest child and a solo mom, I felt like I couldn't afford to sit still. Sitting still meant admitting defeat, and defeat wasn't an option. I was like Sophia from *The Golden Girls* when she said, "I'm 80. I'm supposed to be exhausted." Except I wasn't 80, and I was still exhausted!

But here's the thing: all this constant motion, this perpetual busyness, it's not just exhausting – it's downright counterproductive. It's like trying to run a marathon without ever stopping for water. Sure, you might cover a lot of ground at first, but eventually, you're going to collapse.

The Impact of Rest on Organizational Health

Let's talk about rest, friend. Not the kind of rest where you collapse into bed at 2 a.m. after a 16-hour workday, but real, intentional, guilt-free rest. The kind of rest that makes you feel like a million bucks after a hard-earned vacation – refreshed, rejuvenated, and ready to take on the world.

Studies consistently show that well-rested employees are not only more productive but also exhibit higher levels of job satisfaction and lower rates of turnover. We are supposed to get better with age but many of us are so raggedy we look like the food in the food court that's been sitting under the hot light too long. Well, let me tell you, I am too darn fly to look like stale fast food.

In my journey as a leader, I've learned that promoting a restful culture doesn't just mean adding employee wellness programs; it's about integrating rest as a strategic element in achieving business goals. It's about creating an environment where taking breaks is not just allowed but celebrated.

Think about it: when was the last time you had a brilliant idea while staring bleary-eyed at your computer screen at midnight?

Probably never. But I bet you've had plenty of "aha" moments in the shower, on a walk, or while chatting with friends over brunch.

Leading by Example: The Blueprint for Change

Now, I know what you're thinking. "Kishshana, that sounds great, but how do I actually make this happen?" Well, my friend, it starts with us. As leaders, we need to be the change we want to see. It's like Dwayne Wayne from *A Different World* with his flip-up glasses – we need to flip our perspective on rest.

When I first started implementing rest into my routine, I felt guilty. I mean, shouldn't I be working? Isn't there always more to do? But as I reflected on the number of my contemporaries who had passed away from stress, heart diseases, and more, I realized if I wasn't careful I'd look up and realize that I'd never slowed down to enjoy my hard work. Or worse, I wouldn't look up at all. That hit me like a ton of bricks. I didn't want to reach the end of my life and regret not taking time to rest and enjoy it.

So, I started small. I began by taking actual lunch breaks away from my desk. I set boundaries around my work hours and stuck to them. I took email off my phone for years. I put up a permanent "out-of-office message" that gave folks details about how to access me. I took a break from executive committee work for my sorority. I stepped down from various boards. And you know what? The world didn't end. In fact, things started to improve. My team became more productive, more creative, and happier overall. My relationships, both personal and professional, improved. I even had time to get certified as a wellness coach and am a certified Pilates mat instructor. Next up? Pole dancing!

I had to continually activate my own five-star wellness plan. I realized that it wasn't just about having more free time or feeling less stressed. It was about finding balance and prioritizing what truly mattered to me. I discovered that by taking care of myself, I was able to show up as a better version of myself in all areas of my life.

But it wasn't just about me taking breaks. I had to encourage my team to do the same. I remember one of my employees, let's call her Sarah, was always the last to leave the office. She reminded me of Kim Reese from *A Different World* – always striving to be the best, even at the cost of her own well-being.

One day, I sat her down and channeled my inner Dorothy Zbornak. I said, "Sarah, your work is excellent, but you're burning the candle at both ends. And you know what happens when you do that? You get burned." She looked at me like I had grown a second head, but slowly, she started to understand.

Each of us needs to have a person who is the voice of reason, insisting that sometimes you just need to rest and recharge. Problem is, we've learned to say, "I'm okay, I'm just BUSY" instead of "I'm not okay. I am drowning. What I really need is [insert what you need]." You need someone that can say "let's take a break." That's the kind of leadership we need – one that knows when to pause and encourage others to do the same.

Let's take another quick walk in my shoes. Close your eyes and imagine that you're the first in your family to step foot on a college campus as a student. The weight of expectations – both your own and your family's – sits heavy on your shoulders. That's how I felt on my first day moving into my dorm room at Bentley College (now Bentley University), overwhelmed and unsure, much like many organizations feel when faced with the challenge of implementing systematic rest.

But here's the thing I learned: just as I had to redefine success for myself, companies need to rethink their entire organizational ethos. It's not just about policy changes; it's about a complete mindset shift.

I remember when I called home during my first finals week, exhausted and on the verge of burnout. That's when my mom, one of the hardest-working women I know said, "Kish, even the hardest workers need to rest." It's a lesson that leaders in every industry need to take to heart.

Creating policies for regular breaks, flexible schedules, and periods of disconnection isn't just paperwork – it's a lifeline. But here's the kicker: just like how I had to see my professors using office hours to believe it was okay, employees need to see their leaders practicing these policies. It's not enough to talk the talk; you've got to walk the walk.

The benefits? They're as transformative as my college experience. Boosted morale, reduced burnout, and a more inclusive environment where every employee feels as valued as I did when my family celebrated my graduation. These aren't just nice-to-haves; they're the building blocks of a thriving modern business.

And let's talk about diversity, equity, inclusion, and belonging (DEIB). As a first-generation college student, I know firsthand how crucial it is to feel like you belong. By championing DEIB in rest and recuperation practices, leaders can ensure that everyone, regardless of their background, feels supported and energized to bring their best selves to work.

So, let's take a page from my college journey and embrace the power of rest. After all, sometimes doing less really is the key to achieving more. Are you ready to rewrite your organization's story?

Cultivating a Restful Culture

Creating a culture of rest isn't just about taking more naps (although, let's be honest, who doesn't love a good nap?). It's about fundamentally changing how we view work and productivity. It's about understanding that rest isn't the opposite of work – it's an essential part of it.

Cultivating a restful culture begins with leadership commitment and trickles down to every level of the organization. Let's explore how embracing breaks can transform your workplace into a thriving hub of productivity and well-being.

In today's fast-paced work environment, the idea of rest can sometimes be misconstrued as a hindrance to productivity. However, the truth is quite the opposite. A culture that values rest and encourages breaks can significantly enhance productivity and organizational health. Research[1] shows that employees who take regular breaks are more focused, creative, and efficient in their work. By allowing time for rest, individuals can recharge their energy levels, leading to improved performance overall.

In my company, we've implemented what I like to call the "Golden Girls Rule." Just like how the girls always made time for cheesecake and conversation, we make sure to have regular team breaks. These aren't just quick coffee runs; they're opportunities for us to connect, recharge, and sometimes even solve problems we've been stuck on.

We've adopted a flexible work schedule, understanding that everyone's peak productivity hours are different. Some of us are early birds like Rose, while others are night owls like Blanche. We've also had summer hours for years (when we close on Fridays from June through September). By allowing people to work when they're at their best, we've seen a significant increase in both productivity and job satisfaction.

But perhaps the most important change has been in how we talk about rest. We've made it a point to celebrate rest just as much as we celebrate hard work. When someone takes a well-deserved vacation, we don't grumble about the extra work – we cheer them on. When someone sets healthy boundaries, we applaud them.

---

[1] Wang, Y., & Hsu, Y. (2020). The impact of break time on employee performance: A meta-analysis. *Journal of Applied Psychology*, 105(3), 275–290.

In *A Different World,* Whitley Gilbert might have been known for her high-maintenance ways, but she had a point when she insisted on her beauty sleep and spa days. Self-care wasn't just about looking good; it was about feeling good and performing at her best. Leaders need to take a page out of Whitley's book and prioritize rest to keep their teams at peak performance.

Moreover, a restful culture fosters innovation and problem-solving. When individuals step away from their work for short periods, they allow their minds to wander and make new connections. This mental downtime is essential for creativity to flourish. By encouraging employees to take breaks and engage in activities that promote relaxation, organizations can unlock new ideas and approaches to challenges, leading to increased innovation and growth.

It's like what Whitley Gilbert said in *A Different World*: "I'm the baddest in the school, the baddest in the game." Well, we want our team to be the baddest in the game, too, and that means being well rested and ready to take on any challenge.

The Effects of C-PTSD on Work Patterns

Now, let's get real for a moment. For many of us, especially those of us who have experienced trauma or live with chronic stress, rest isn't just about taking a break – it's about healing. As someone who has dealt with C-PTSD (complex post-traumatic stress disorder), I know firsthand how this can affect work patterns.

For years, I used work as a way to avoid dealing with my trauma. I was like Sophia when she said, "I'm an old lady. I'm supposed to be colorful." Except instead of being colorful, I was just constantly busy.

I filled every moment with work, thinking that if I just kept moving, the pain couldn't catch up to me.

But here's the thing about trauma – it doesn't just go away because you ignore it. It shows up in our work patterns, in our relationships, in the way we treat ourselves. For me, it manifested as an inability to slow down, a constant need to prove my worth through productivity.

It took me a long time to realize that true healing couldn't happen without rest. Just like how the Golden Girls always came together to support each other through tough times, I had to learn to be there for myself. I had to learn that taking time to rest and process wasn't a luxury; it was a necessity.

Playing Burnout Bingo

Alright, let's talk about burnout in a way that'll make you laugh and cry at the same time – because if we're not laughing, we're crying, right?

A day in the life of a struggling professional trying to hold on to your sanity is like holding on to a twister ride at an amusement park. You're dealing with endless emails, back-to-back meetings, and a to-do list longer than the line for ticket sales to the next Beyoncé tour. You're starting to feel like you're losing your mind.

I call it "Burnout Bingo." Here's how you play:

1. Stare blankly at your computer screen for 10 minutes straight? Check!

2. Forget what day it is … again? Bingo!

3. Consider faking a tropical disease to get out of work? You're on fire!

4. Fantasize about telling your boss to "shove it" in increasingly creative ways? Now we're talking!

5. Realize you've been wearing the same sweatpants for a week? Congratulations, you've won!

But seriously, folks, burnout is no joke. It's like being stuck in a never-ending episode of *A Different World,* where you're Dwayne Wayne, and your flip-up glasses are permanently stuck in the "I can't deal with this" position.

Research[2] shows that burnout can lead to a whole host of problems, from physical health issues to mental health concerns. It's like your body and mind are staging a revolt, and trust me, it's not the fun kind of revolt where you get to eat cake and overthrow the monarchy.

So, what can we do about it? Well, for starters, you can try the Golden Girls approach to stress relief:

1. Eat cheesecake at 2 a.m.

2. Deliver witty one-liners.

3. Have a group of sassy friends to commiserate with.

But if that doesn't work (and let's face it, not all of us can pull off shoulder pads like Blanche), you might need to get a bit more creative.

How about instituting a "Burnout Buzzer" at work? Whenever someone's reaching their limit, they hit the buzzer, and everyone has to stop what they're doing and engage in a mandatory dance party. It's hard to feel stressed when you're doing the robot, right?

Or maybe we could introduce "Reverse Performance Reviews," where employees get to evaluate their bosses on how well they're preventing burnout. "Sorry, Bob, but your 'motivational' emails at

---

[2] Pencavel, J. (2014). The productivity of working hours. *The Economic Journal, 124*(581), 205–227.

11 p.m. are not cutting it. We're going to need you to step up your game and maybe learn how to use emojis."

In all seriousness, though, addressing burnout is crucial. Remember, it's okay to take breaks, set boundaries, and prioritize your mental health. After all, you can't pour from an empty cup, even if that cup is full of your favorite beverage.

So, the next time you feel burnout creeping in, take that as an opportunity to dance, evaluate your work-life balance, and maybe even have a conversation with your boss about implementing strategies to prevent burnout. Because let's face it, no one wants to be the one doing the robot at a mandatory "fun" office party. One way to combat burnout is by incorporating fun activities into the workday. This can include team-building exercises, group lunches, or even just taking a few minutes to play a game with coworkers. Not only will this break up the monotony of work but it can also improve morale and create a more positive work environment.

Signs You're Approaching Burnout

Because many of us are so used to running on *E* that we don't know when it's time to rest, here are a few signs that it might be time to take a breather:

- **You're making careless mistakes:** If you're usually detail-oriented but suddenly find yourself making silly errors, it might be time for a break.

- **You're irritable:** If every little thing is getting on your nerves (queue the fingerprints on the walls or the "honey-do" list that hasn't been touched in weeks), it's probably time to step back.

- **You're having trouble focusing:** If your mind is wandering more than Rose during one of her long-winded stories, it's a sign you need some rest.

- **You're not enjoying things you usually love:** I know that when my molten chocolate lava cake doesn't hit the spot; it's definitely time for a break.

- **You're neglecting your five-star wellness plan:** If you can't remember the last time you did something just for you, it's time to channel your inner Blanche and pamper yourself a little.

Remember, taking time to rest isn't selfish – it's necessary. I can hear my dad saying to me, "You can't help anybody if you don't help yourself first."

Conclusion: Embracing the Power of Rest

As I wrap up this chapter, I'm reminded of something Sophia once said: "I'm 80. I'm tired. Good night." Although we might not all be 80 (thank goodness), we all get tired. And that's okay. In fact, it's more than okay; it's human.

Learning to rest before you act isn't just about avoiding burnout. It's about giving yourself the space to grow, to create, to be your best self. It's about understanding that productivity isn't about how many hours you work, but about the quality of work you produce when you're at your best.

So, the next time you feel like you need to push through, remember this: even the Golden Girls took breaks for cheesecake. Even the students at Hillman College had downtime between classes. And you, my friend, deserve that same kind of rest.

As we move forward in this fast-paced world, let's make a pact to prioritize rest. Let's be the leaders who show that it's not just okay to take breaks; it's essential. Let's create workplaces where rest is celebrated, where self-care is encouraged, and where we all have the opportunity to be our best selves.

Because at the end of the day, life isn't about how busy you are. It's about how fulfilled you are. And trust me, you can't be truly fulfilled if you're running on empty.

So go ahead, take that break. Rest before you act. And who knows? You might just find that when you do act, you're capable of more than you ever imagined. After all, as Blanche would say, "There is a fine line between having a good time and being a wagon-wheeled buffoon." Let's make sure we're on the right side of that line, shall we?

CHAPTER 10

FROM BUSY BEE TO
QUEEN BEE

MASTERING WORK-LIFE SYNERGY

"My mission in life is not merely to survive, but to thrive; and to do so with some passion, some compassion, some humor, and some style."

MAYA ANGELOU

This chapter explores how our childhood experiences, particularly those of us who were latch-key kids, have shaped our adult tendencies toward busyness. I examine why we feel the need to constantly be in motion, and more important, how we can break free from this cycle of exhaustion. It's time to reclaim the peace we once found in those quiet after-school hours and learn to thrive without running on fumes.

So, let's take a journey back to those formative years and see how they've influenced our present. It's time to unlock the door to a more balanced, fulfilling life – no shoelace required.

Growing Up a Latch-Key Kid in Queens

I grew up in Queens, New York, nestled within the sprawling urban landscape of New York City. Queens is a borough rich with vibrant culture and stark contrasts. Queens offered a unique blend of diverse communities, each with its own distinct character. The streets were alive with the sounds of hip-hop's infancy, echoing from boomboxes on stoops, while graffiti art began to transform dull city walls into canvases of bold expression. Amidst this backdrop, children played football in the streets and families gathered in kitchens where recipes passed down through generations filled the air with enticing aromas.

This environment, marked by its resilience and creativity, shaped the dreams and ambitions of those who called it home. Queens was a place where anything seemed possible, and its energy fueled the passions of its inhabitants. At eight years old, I had a house key tied around my neck with a shoelace. My stepdad dropped me off in the front of our building and I hurried upstairs. Outside, the streets of Jamaica, Queens, bustled with life – the smell of fresh hardo bread from the Jamaican bakery mingling with the honks of impatient taxi drivers. But for me, that key represented a world of independence and responsibility that most kids my age couldn't fathom.

As I turned the lock and stepped into the quiet emptiness of our apartment, I felt a mix of pride and loneliness. My parents, like so many others in our neighborhood, worked long hours to provide for our family. Their absence meant I had to keep myself busy and out of trouble until they returned.

I'd raid the fridge for an after-school snack, usually settling for a peanut butter and jelly sandwich and a glass of milk. Then, I'd spread my homework across the kitchen table, determined to finish it before my mom came home. Once I was done, I'd retreat to my room to read my favorite authors under the covers with a flashlight. I was always moving. Singing, writing, commanding my dolls at home and my friends at school. But as I grew older, I began to realize that my love for constant stimulation stemmed from wanting to escape the quiet emptiness of our apartment – even though I wasn't alone (my brother was my first best friend, singing partner, and sidekick). Our neighborhood was not the safest, and it was often plagued by violence and crime. My parents shielded me from most of it, but all the kids talked about it at school.

As I got older, I'd venture out to the mini shopping center that was right next to our building. Or I'd head to the library to check out another book. As the sun began to set and the street lights flickered on, I'd make sure I was inside, locking the door behind me. I'd get ready for dinner, keeping one ear tuned for the sound of my parents' key in the lock.

Looking back, my childhood shaped me in ways I'm only now beginning to understand. The independence I cultivated as a latch-key kid became the foundation for my adult life – a life where busyness is worn like a badge of honor and running on fumes is practically a competitive sport.

It's as if those childhood years of self-reliance programmed me to constantly seek out tasks, to fill every moment with activity. The quiet moments that once stretched endlessly in my childhood home now feel almost unbearable. I find myself constantly on the go, juggling work, social commitments, and personal projects with the same determination I once applied to finishing my homework before *DuckTales* came on.

But here's the thing – just like that eight-year-old with a house key, we're all trying to unlock something. For many of us, it's the secret to feeling fulfilled, successful, or simply good enough. We run ourselves ragged, thinking that if we just do one more thing, achieve one more goal, we'll finally feel complete.

Growing up as a latch-key kid in Queens during the 1980s and 1990s, especially as a child of immigrant parents, was an experience that profoundly shaped my perspective on work ethic, work-life balance, and rest. The unique challenges we faced as Gen X kids of immigrant parents influenced our relationship with work and rest in several significant ways. Even if you aren't the child of immigrant parents, I'm curious if you see parts of yourself in what I am about to describe.

Witnessing Sacrifice and Hard Work

My parents came to the United States with dreams of a better life, often taking on grueling jobs that required long hours and immense physical labor. My parents, like many others, worked tirelessly to provide for our family. This relentless work ethic was not just about survival; it was about creating opportunities for their children that they themselves never had.

Growing up, I saw my parents leave the house before dawn and return late at night, exhausted but determined. Their sacrifices instilled in me a deep respect for hard work and a belief that success comes from relentless effort and perseverance. This was a common narrative among children of immigrants, who often felt a profound sense of duty to honor their parents' sacrifices by excelling in school and later in their careers.

Balancing Multiple Roles

As latch-key kids, we had to balance multiple roles from a young age. We were students, caregivers, and sometimes even translators for our parents, who might have struggled with English. This early exposure to responsibility taught us to be resourceful and independent. We learned to manage our time efficiently, juggling homework, household chores, and sometimes part-time jobs to contribute to the family income.

Pressure to Succeed

The pressure to succeed was immense. Our parents often had high expectations, pushing us toward careers in medicine, law, engineering, or business – fields they believed would offer financial security and prestige. This pressure was a double-edged sword: it motivated us to strive for excellence but also created a fear of failure and a relentless drive to be constantly productive.

The Impact on Work-Life Balance

The concept of work-life balance has become increasingly crucial in our modern, technology-driven world. It refers to the delicate equilibrium between personal and professional activities, essential for reducing stress and enhancing overall well-being. My own understanding of this balance has been profoundly shaped by my upbringing, a realization that only dawned on me as I began to critically examine my approach to work and life.

Our work ethic, which significantly affects our ability to achieve work-life balance, is deeply rooted in our formative years. Research indicates that parents play a pivotal role in molding our attitudes toward work. The quality of our relationships with our parents during adolescence can have lasting effects on our work values and orientations. Moreover, cultural context adds another layer of influence, often dictating different perspectives on work and success.

Constant Busyness

The work ethic instilled in me by my immigrant parents often translated into a constant state of busyness. I equated being busy with being productive and successful. This mindset carried over into my adult life, where I felt the need to fill every moment with activity, often running on fumes and neglecting rest.

Struggle with Rest and Self-Care

For many of us, rest and self-care are foreign concepts. My parents rarely took time off, and the idea of self-care was often seen as a luxury I couldn't afford. This mentality made it difficult for me to prioritize my own well-being. I initially felt guilty taking breaks, fearing it would be seen as laziness or lack of ambition.

Redefining Success

As I grew older, I began to question the traditional definitions of success that I inherited from my parents. I started to value work-life balance and personal fulfillment over mere financial success. This shift was not always easy, as it sometimes meant defying my parents' expectations and carving out new paths that aligned more closely with my own values and aspirations.

The WAY WAY UPSIDE

I have to pause here to say, it wasn't all doom and gloom. I experienced a lot of challenges but also a lot of joy. And my parents' work ethic rubbed off; I never had trouble finding a job and performed well in my career. But what I realized was that success meant something different to me than it did to them. It wasn't just

(continued)

From Busy Bee to Queen Bee

(continued)

about climbing the corporate ladder or making a certain amount of money. It was about finding fulfillment and balance in all areas of life (don't tell Mama Dawn, but she was right).

This realization has led many of Gen Xers, trained and mentored by boomers, and millennials, tired of the status quo, to redefine success for themselves, focusing on holistic well-being rather than traditional markers of achievement. We have shifted our priorities toward work-life balance, mental and emotional health, and personal growth.

As we continue to navigate our careers, we are challenging societal expectations and norms by prioritizing our own well-being over external measures of success. My parents and my cultural background taught me that success meant climbing the corporate ladder and making a certain amount of money. However, I have learned that true fulfillment comes from finding balance and happiness in all aspects of my life, not just my job title or salary.

This realization has been especially prevalent among Gen Xers like me who were raised and trained by boomers. We have seen the toll that the traditional definition of success can take on individuals, as well as its lack of sustainability and personal fulfillment. So instead, we are choosing to redefine success for ourselves.

We are prioritizing work-life balance, mental and emotional health, and personal growth over constantly chasing external markers of achievement. This might mean taking time off to travel or to spend with family, pursuing hobbies outside of work, or even switching careers to something that aligns more with our passions and values.

But this shift in mindset doesn't mean we are not driven or ambitious. In fact, it's quite the opposite. By taking care of ourselves and finding balance in all aspects of life, we are able to show up as

Busy Is A Four-Letter Word

our best selves in both personal and professional settings. We are able to achieve success on our own terms without sacrificing our well-being.

This new approach to success is also reflected in how we view money and material possessions. Although they can provide temporary happiness, we have learned that true fulfillment comes from experiences and relationships rather than accumulating stuff.

As Gen Xers continue to navigate through the changing landscape of work culture and redefine success for themselves, their unique perspectives and values will continue to make a significant impact on society. So let's not shy away from our "slacker" reputation, but instead embrace it as a key component of our balanced and fulfilling lives.

I'm a Boss

Here are some key ways that being an immigrant or child of immigrants has shaped my leadership style:

- **Vision and determination:** My parents had a clear vision for their future and demonstrated strong determination to achieve their goals. This translates into leadership that is focused on long-term objectives and perseveres through challenges.

- **Adaptability and resilience:** The immigrant experience requires adapting to new cultures, languages, and systems. This fosters resilience and flexibility in leadership, enabling me to navigate change and uncertainty more effectively.

- **Embracing diversity:** Growing up in diverse communities or experiencing different cultures firsthand often leads to leadership that values and leverages diversity. I am more comfortable with multicultural teams and can bridge cultural differences.

- **Strong work ethic:** Many immigrants come from backgrounds where hard work is highly valued. For me, this often translates to a style of leadership that leads by example and sets high standards for effort and dedication.

- **Innovative problem-solving:** Facing unique challenges in a new country often requires creative solutions. I learned early that I think outside the box and approach problems from multiple angles.

- **Empathy and inclusivity:** Understanding the struggles of being an outsider has made me more empathetic and inclusive. I am highly attuned to the needs of marginalized groups and work to create inclusive environments wherever I go.

- **Global perspective:** Spending all my summers in Jamaica, West Indies, and even living in Budapest, Hungary, in high school shifted the way I saw and understood people who didn't look like me. Exposure to different cultures and ways of thinking gave me a more global perspective.

- **Emphasis on education and growth:** My parents and ALL my friends' parents placed a high value on education as a path to success. So now I am a champion for leadership that prioritizes continuous learning and development for themselves and their teams.

- **Humility and openness to learning:** The experience of having to learn new systems and cultures can instill a sense of humility and openness to learning in children of immigrants. It took some time, but now I am more willing to admit what I don't know and seek input from others.

- **Strong communication skills:** Navigating language barriers and explaining oneself in new contexts can hone communication skills. I learned early to be able to communicate effectively across cultures and with diverse audiences.

Embracing the Power of the Strategic No

Remember when Blanche Devereaux would say yes to every man who asked her out? Although that might work for dating (that's debatable), it's a recipe for disaster in our professional life and personal life. Learning to say no strategically is like finding the perfect red velvet cake recipe; it takes practice, but once you master it, life becomes so much sweeter.

As leaders, we often feel pressured to take on every project, attend every meeting, and be available 24/7. But here's a little secret: saying yes to everything means you're saying no to something else, often your own well-being or quality time with loved ones.

I remember when I first started my company. I was like Dwayne Wayne trying to impress Whitley – saying yes to every client, every speaking engagement, every networking event. I thought being busy meant I was successful. But you know what? I was exhausted, cranky, and my work was suffering. I had to learn to channel my inner Sophia and start telling it like it is: "No, I can't take on that project right now," or "No, that meeting doesn't align with my current priorities."

It wasn't easy at first. I felt the mom guilt, the working parent guilt, the people-pleasing urge to make everyone happy. But then I realized something important: by saying no to things that didn't align with my values or goals, I was saying yes to myself and the things that truly mattered.

Here's a little exercise for you: think about the last time you said yes to something you really didn't want to do. How did it make you feel? Now, imagine if you had said no instead. What could you have done with that time and energy? Maybe you could have finished that important project, spent quality time with your family, or (gasp) actually gotten a full night's sleep!

Learning to say no strategically isn't about being selfish. It's about being intentional with your time and energy. It's about prioritizing what's truly important and letting go of the rest. And friend, I don't want to hear that you cannot. Actually, you can. It's time to take control of your life and your schedule.

From Disciplinarian to Advisor: The Evolution of Leadership

Now, let's talk about how leadership has evolved, both in parenting and in the workplace. Leadership, much like parenting, has undergone a significant transformation. Gone are the days when leaders were mere disciplinarians, barking orders from atop their ivory towers. Today, leaders are more akin to advisors, guiding their teams with empathy and understanding. This shift mirrors the evolution of parenting from the strict disciplinarian approach to the more nurturing and advisory role.

Remember when parents (and bosses) were all about "Because I said so!" and "Do as I say, not as I do"? Well, times have changed, and thank goodness for that!

In the world of parenting, we've moved from the authoritarian *Father Knows Best* model to a more gentle, authoritative approach. There is a marked difference between my strict West Indian upbringing and the way I raised my own child – with a bit more understanding and a lot more communication.

This shift in parenting styles mirrors what's happening in the workplace. We're moving away from the directive, top-down approach of management to a more collaborative, coaching style of leadership. It's less about barking orders and more about empowering your team to find solutions.

I remember when I first became a manager. I thought I had to have all the answers and tell everyone exactly what to do. So I became bossy, controlling, and frankly, a bit of a nightmare. But then I had my own "aha" moment (and thank goodness for that), I realized that my job wasn't to have all the answers, but to ask the right questions and guide my team to find their own solutions.

> **Note:** The shift from disciplinarian to advisor isn't just about being nice. It's about creating a supportive work environment where people feel valued, heard, and empowered. It's about fostering creativity, innovation, and personal growth. And let me tell you, when you create that kind of environment, magic happens.

Here's an example: I had an employee who was struggling with time management. Instead of reprimanding her or micromanaging her schedule, I sat down with her and asked, "What's getting in your way? How can we work together to find a solution?" We had an open, honest conversation about her challenges and brainstormed strategies to help her be more effective. Not only did her performance improve, but she felt supported and valued, which increased her overall job satisfaction.

This approach to leadership isn't just about being a nice boss. It's about creating a culture of trust, growth, and mutual respect. It's about recognizing that your team members are whole people with lives outside of work and recognizing their humanity.

Cultivating Supportive Work Environments: The Cheesecake Approach

Speaking of humanity, let's talk about creating a work environment that feels less like a cold, corporate machine and more like a warm, inviting kitchen where problems are solved over slices of cheesecake.

In *The Golden Girls,* the kitchen was the heart of the home. It was where the ladies gathered to share their triumphs, their struggles, and, of course, their cheesecake. Now, I'm not saying you need to install a cheesecake bar in your office (although, that's not a bad idea), but you do need to create spaces and opportunities for your team to connect, share, and support each other.

This is where the concept of work-life synergy comes into play. It's not about achieving perfect balance – let's face it, perfect balance is about as real as Rose's St. Olaf stories. Instead, it's about creating an environment where work and life can coexist harmoniously.

Here are a few ways you can cultivate a supportive work environment:

- **Flexible work arrangements:** Channel your inner Blanche and be open to new experiences. Offer flexible hours or remote work options when possible. This enables your team to manage their personal responsibilities while still getting their work done.

- **Open communication:** Create an atmosphere where people feel comfortable sharing their challenges and asking for help. Remember how the Golden Girls could always count on each other? That's the kind of support system you want to foster in your workplace.

- **Encourage breaks and self-care:** Dorothy wouldn't let Sophia overexert herself, and you shouldn't let your team burn out either. Encourage regular breaks, promote wellness activities, and lead by example in prioritizing self-care.

- **Celebrate successes:** Take a page from Blanche's book and don't be shy about celebrating wins, big and small. Recognition goes a long way in creating a positive work environment.

- **Promote learning and growth:** Like Dwayne Wayne's journey from class clown to successful lawyer, provide opportunities for your team to learn, grow, and advance in their careers.

Remember, a supportive work environment isn't just about being nice; it's about creating a space where people can thrive, both professionally and personally. It's about recognizing that your team members are whole people with lives outside of work, and that supporting their overall well-being will ultimately lead to better results for everyone.

Measuring Success Holistically: Beyond the Bottom Line

Now, let's talk about success. In the business world, we often get caught up in numbers – profits, key performance indicators and metrics. It's like Blanche focusing solely on the number of men she's dated. But just as Blanche learned that true happiness came from quality relationships, not quantity, we need to learn to measure success more holistically.

In *A Different World,* success wasn't just about grades. It was about personal growth, community impact, and finding one's place in the world. The same should be true in our workplaces. Success isn't just about meeting targets or increasing profits. It's about creating value – for our customers, our employees, our communities, and ourselves.

So, how do you measure success holistically? Here are a few ideas:

- **Employee satisfaction and well-being:** Happy employees are productive employees. Regularly check in with your team about their job satisfaction, stress levels, and overall well-being.
- **Personal and professional growth:** Hold your team members accountable for cocreating their professional development

and measure how your team members are growing and developing their skills.

- **Work-life synergy:** Assess how well your team members are able to integrate their work and personal lives. Are they able to attend important family events? Do they have time for hobbies and self-care?

- **Community impact:** Consider how your organization is contributing to the wider community. Are you making a positive difference?

- **Customer satisfaction:** Beyond just sales numbers, how happy are your customers? Are you creating real value for them?

- **Innovation and creativity:** Are you fostering an environment where new ideas can flourish?

Remember, success isn't a destination; it's a journey. It's about continuous improvement and growth, both for individuals and for the organization as a whole. It's about creating a workplace where people don't just survive but thrive.

Mastering Work-Life Synergy: *The Golden Girls* Guide

Now, I know what you're thinking. "Kishshana, that's easier said than done!" And you're right. But I believe that change is possible if you're willing to put in the work.

So, let's talk about how we can go from busy bees to queen bees, mastering the art of work-life synergy. Because life isn't about balance, my friends. It's about integration, communication, and making choices that align with our values. It's time to stop trying to have it all and start deciding what "all" means to you.

Now, let's bring it all together and talk about mastering work-life synergy. This isn't about achieving perfect balance. As Sophia would say, "Picture it: Sicily, 1922. Balance was for tightrope walkers and people who didn't know how to live!" Instead, it's about creating a life where your work and personal lives complement and enhance each other, rather than compete.

Here's how you can master work-life synergy, Golden Girls style:

- **Define your values:** Like how each of the Golden Girls had their own unique personality and priorities, identify what's truly important to you. Is it family time? Career advancement? Personal hobbies? Once you know your values, you can align your choices accordingly.

- **Set boundaries:** Blanche knew how to say no to a date (rarely, but she could). Learn to set boundaries in your work life. This might mean not checking emails after a certain time or blocking off time in your calendar for personal activities.

- **Prioritize self-care:** Dorothy always made sure to take care of herself, whether it was with a good book or a witty comeback. Make self-care a non-negotiable part of your routine.

- **Cultivate supportive relationships:** The Golden Girls' strength came from their friendship. Build a support network both at work and in your personal life.

- **Embrace flexibility:** Life doesn't always go according to plan (just ask Rose about some of her St. Olaf stories). Be willing to adjust and adapt as needed.

- **Practice mindfulness:** Be present in the moment, whether you're at work or at home. As Sophia would say, "Why do today what you can put off until tomorrow? Because you might die tonight, that's why!"

- **Celebrate the small wins:** Whether it's finishing a project at work or making it to your kid's soccer game, take time to acknowledge and celebrate your achievements.

Remember, work-life synergy isn't about having it all; it's about having what matters most to you. It's about creating a life that feels fulfilling and authentic, both in and out of the office.

Conclusion: From Busy Bee to Queen Bee

As I wrap up this chapter, I want you to think about the transformation from busy bee to queen bee. A busy bee flits from flower to flower, always in motion but not always productive. A queen bee, however, is purposeful, strategic, and essential to the health of the entire hive.

By embracing the power of the strategic no, evolving your leadership style, cultivating a supportive work environment, measuring success holistically, and mastering work-life synergy, you can transform from a busy bee to a queen bee. You can create a life and a leadership style that's not just busy, but truly effective and fulfilling.

Remember, as Dorothy would say, "You're not just a woman, Barbara. You're a person. And you have a right to a life of your own." The same is true for you, whether you're Barbara, Bob, or anyone in between. You have the right to a life that's not just busy, but truly meaningful.

So, the next time someone asks you how you're doing, resist the urge to say "busy." Instead, channel your inner Golden Girl or your favorite character from *A Different World*. Be honest, be authentic, and be proud of the life you're creating – a life where work and personal time coexist harmoniously, where success is measured in more than just dollars and cents, and where you're not just surviving, but truly thriving.

Now, if you'll excuse me, I have a date with a cheesecake and some reruns of *The Golden Girls*. After all, part of work-life synergy is knowing when to take a break and enjoy the sweeter things in life. Thank you for being a friend on this journey from busy bee to queen bee. Remember, life is short, eat dessert first, and never be too busy to laugh, love, and live your best life.

CHAPTER 11

CULTIVATING YOUR CIRCLE:
THE STRENGTH IN SUPPORTIVE
NETWORKS

"Find a group of people who challenge and inspire you; spend a lot of time with them, and it will change your life."

AMY POEHLER

In an era when busy has become not just a status but a lifestyle, it's pivotal to reevaluate how you manage your professional relationships. The essence of building a supportive professional network transcends the mere accumulation of contacts; it involves cultivating meaningful connections that bolster both personal and professional growth. This chapter delves into why nurturing these relationships is crucial, how to effectively collaborate and delegate within these networks, and how to develop systems that support sharing workloads, ultimately enhancing productivity and fulfillment.

Previous chapters explored various strategies to escape the trap of chronic busyness – from prioritizing tasks effectively to harnessing the power of saying no. This chapter transitions into discussing professional networks. It will become clear that these are not just complementary strategies but are central to transforming how you work. By shifting focus from individual accomplishment to collective success, you can create an environment where productivity is not just about doing more but about achieving more through shared effort.

The importance of a supportive network cannot be overstated. It provides not just emotional backing but also practical assistance in navigating career challenges. A robust network offers diverse viewpoints and skills, enabling problem-solving from various angles and fostering innovative thinking. This diversity not only enriches the solutions but also embeds a deeper sense of inclusion and belonging within professional environments.

Engaging in effective collaboration and delegation is another cornerstone of maximizing productivity. This involves recognizing the unique strengths of individuals within your network and leveraging these for collective success. Effective delegation isn't merely about offloading tasks; it's about entrusting colleagues with responsibilities that suit their expertise, thereby boosting efficiency and job satisfaction across the board.

Cultivating Your Circle: The Strength in Supportive Networks

Moreover, developing a system for sharing workloads – what I call *lifeloads* – is essential for sustaining long-term productivity without reaching burnout. Such systems ensure that work is distributed fairly and that no single person is overwhelmed, aligning perfectly with the overarching goal of achieving more by doing less. These strategies not only optimize output but also contribute to a healthier, more balanced work environment.

As you reflect on the different approaches to doing less so you can achieve more, remember that (like all the other strategies and tactics you have walked through up to this point) these networking strategies are integral to the broader goal: reshaping your approach to work and life to escape the relentless cycle of busyness. By building and engaging with your networks thoughtfully, you can enhance your immediate productivity and set the stage for sustained personal and professional growth.

Unleashing the Power of Networks: A Strategic Blueprint for Thriving

If you were a friend I hadn't seen in a while and I couldn't get on the phone but I KNOW you check your email, I might send you this:

> *Hey, friend! I know it's been a while since we've had a chance to catch up, and I can imagine how busy you've been. But I wanted to share something that's been on my mind about how we can all do less and achieve more.*
>
> *You know how sometimes it feels like we're just running on a hamster wheel, doing everything on our own and still not getting anywhere? Well, I've been learning that building a strong, supportive network can make all the difference. It's not just about having a bunch of contacts; it's about creating*

meaningful relationships that really help us grow and succeed together. Think about it like this: instead of trying to tackle everything solo, imagine having a few trusted friends and colleagues who are there to share the load, offer advice, and open up new opportunities. It's like having a team of superheroes by your side! These connections can turn everyday tasks into chances for growth and make our professional lives so much more fulfilling and less stressful. It's all about moving away from the hustle culture, where being "busy" is a badge of honor, and instead, embracing a smarter, more collaborative approach. Trust me, it's a game changer. Let's catch up soon and talk more about this! I can't wait to hear how these ideas resonate with you and see how they can help us both find more balance and joy in our work.

So, as you go through this chapter, I hope you'll find some practical tips on how to build these valuable relationships.

Thomas's Story

In the dim light of a late afternoon, the cafe hummed with the murmur of conversations and the clink of coffee cups. Thomas sat at his usual corner table, a stronghold amidst the chaos, his laptop open but ignored for the moment. He pondered over his recent project at work, a complex task requiring more hands than were available in his current team.

The aroma of roasted coffee beans mingled with the scent of rain that had started to tap gently against the window. Thomas watched as people, umbrellas in hand, hastened by. His mind wandered back to last week's meeting where his proposal was met with

(continued)

(continued)

enthusiasm but also a hint of skepticism from his superiors. They questioned his capacity to manage such an ambitious project.

His thoughts were interrupted as Jessica, a colleague and part of his professional network, approached with her tray. "Mind if I join you?" she asked, her presence pulling him back from the brink of professional doubt.

"Please," he gestured to the empty seat across from him. As she settled down, her ease contrasted starkly with his inner turmoil.

Jessica was always efficient in her role, someone Thomas admired for her ability to delegate effectively within her team. She sipped her coffee before noticing Thomas's furrowed brow. "You look like you're trying to solve world hunger," she joked lightly.

Thomas chuckled despite himself but then shared his concerns about handling the new project alongside other responsibilities. Jessica listened intently, nodding occasionally.

"You need a better system for sharing these workloads," she advised after he finished explaining. "Why not leverage our network more? There are many here who could offer not just help but also guidance."

The idea struck Thomas like a splash of cold water. Of course! Why hadn't he considered this more seriously? His network wasn't just a collection of business cards but a potential goldmine of support and expertise.

As they continued their discussion, Thomas felt a weight lifting off him. The simple act of sharing his concerns had opened up possibilities he hadn't seen before. Jessica shared stories from projects in which collaboration and clear delegation had saved the day – tales that sparked ideas in Thomas's mind about how he could approach his own situation differently.

Outside, the rain had stopped, and a sliver of sunlight broke through the clouds, casting golden hues across their table. It seemed symbolic – a sign perhaps that solutions were never too far away when one had connections to tap into.

When they parted ways, Jessica reminded him that no one has to carry burdens alone if they build and maintain strong relationships within their network. Thomas sat there for several moments after she left, inspired and revitalized by their conversation. He began typing out emails to various contacts he'd underused before – potential collaborators who might share both workload and insights into navigating this complex project successfully.

As he finally closed down his laptop, feeling more hopeful than when he first opened it today at this very table, one question lingered in his mind: how often do we overlook our most accessible resources in times of need?

In today's fast-paced world, where demands are high and time is limited, having a supportive network can make all the difference. Collaboration within your network can help you leverage the strengths of others, share responsibilities, and achieve more together than you could alone. By working together toward common goals, you can accomplish tasks more efficiently and effectively. Delegation is another crucial aspect of building a strong network. Knowing when to pass on tasks to others who are better equipped or have more time can help lighten your workload and prevent burnout.

Embrace Collaboration, Elevate Productivity

Effective collaboration and delegation require trust and clear communication within your network. Open and honest dialogue can foster understanding and prevent misunderstandings. By being transparent about your needs, goals, and limitations, you enable others to support you effectively. Similarly, being attentive to the needs of those in your network shows that you value their contributions and strengthens the bond between you.

> **Tip:** When cultivating your circle of support, it's essential to seek out individuals who bring diverse perspectives and skills to the table. Diversity in your network can lead to more innovative solutions and a broader range of opportunities. Embracing different backgrounds, experiences, and viewpoints can enrich your own understanding and help you navigate challenges with a more well-rounded approach.

Build a Supportive Network: The Fun Way to Do Less and Achieve More

Alright, friend, let's talk about building a professional network that doesn't just help you get ahead but also makes the journey a whole lot more enjoyable. Think of it as creating your own Avengers team – only without the spandex (unless that's your thing, no judgment here).

Reciprocity: The Secret Sauce

First things first, building a supportive network isn't just about what you can get from others. It's also about what you can give. Reciprocity is the name of the game. Offer your support, share your expertise, or lend a hand when someone needs it. It's like a friendship bracelet for grownups – give a little, get a little, and everyone ends up looking fabulous.

Evolving Relationships: Keep It Fresh

Your professional relationships aren't static; they evolve over time. Regular check-ins, a quick coffee catch-up, or even a funny meme can keep those connections strong. Think of it as watering your plants – except these plants can help you get a promotion or land that dream project.

Quality over Quantity

It's not about having a Rolodex (remember those?) full of names. It's about having a few solid, dependable connections. Quality trumps quantity every time. A handful of strong relationships can offer more support and opportunities than 100 superficial ones. It's like preferring a few good friends over 1,000 Facebook acquaintances.

Collaboration: The Magic Word

Collaboration is where the magic happens. Pooling resources, sharing ideas, and tackling challenges together can lead to some pretty amazing results. Plus, working with others brings fresh perspectives and a sense of community. It's like a potluck dinner; everyone brings something different, and together, you create a feast.

Delegation: Share the Load

Delegation isn't just about offloading tasks; it's about trusting others to handle things they're great at, freeing you up to focus on what you do best. It's like being the captain of a ship; you don't need to swab the deck when you've got a crew for that. Trust your network, and let them shine.

Mutual Respect: The Glue That Binds

Mutual respect is the glue that holds your network together. Treat others with respect, acknowledge their expertise, and appreciate their contributions. It's like the golden rule of networking; treat others how you want to be treated, and you'll build a culture of trust and camaraderie.

Communication: Keep It Clear

Clear and open communication is key. Make sure everyone knows what's expected, roles are defined, and feedback is constructive. It's like setting the GPS for a road trip; everyone knows the destination and the best route to get there.

Empathy: The Superpower

Empathy is your secret superpower. Understanding others' perspectives, needs, and challenges enables you to offer meaningful support and encouragement. It's like having a sixth sense for what people need, making your network stronger and more compassionate.

Together We Shine

So, there you have it. Building a supportive professional network is all about collaboration, delegation, respect, communication, and empathy. By leveraging the strengths of your connections and fostering a culture of mutual support, you'll find that you can achieve more together than you ever could alone. Remember, we're all in this together – so let's make it fun, supportive, and wildly successful!

Cultivate Your Circle

In developing a system for sharing workloads and lifeloads and gaining guidance to enhance productivity and fulfillment, it is crucial to establish clear communication channels within your network. Open and honest communication fosters trust and enables effective collaboration. By clearly outlining expectations, sharing goals, and discussing challenges openly, you create a supportive environment where everyone feels heard and valued.

Establishing boundaries is another key aspect of cultivating a healthy network. Setting boundaries helps prevent burnout and ensures that responsibilities are distributed fairly among members. It is essential to communicate your limits and respect the boundaries of others to maintain a balanced dynamic within the group.

Regular check-ins can help keep everyone on track and provide opportunities for feedback and support. Whether through virtual meetings, email updates, or shared project management tools, staying connected with your network ensures that everyone is aligned toward common goals and can offer assistance when needed.

When it comes to sharing workloads, leveraging each other's strengths is paramount. Assign tasks based on individual expertise and interests to maximize efficiency and quality of work. By recognizing and using the unique skills of each member in your network, you create a synergistic environment where everyone contributes meaningfully to the collective success.

Offering guidance within your network is not only about providing advice but also about being a supportive mentor or coach. Sharing knowledge, experiences, and resources can empower others to overcome challenges and grow professionally. By being an active listener and offering constructive feedback, you can help others navigate obstacles more effectively.

In addition to work-related tasks, sharing lifeloads within your network can also contribute to overall well-being and productivity. Supporting each other in personal matters, through emotional support during tough times or practical assistance with daily responsibilities, strengthens the bonds within the group and creates a sense of community beyond professional endeavors.

Embracing diversity within your network is essential for gaining different perspectives and fostering innovation. By including individuals from various backgrounds, experiences, and skill sets, you enrich the collaborative process and expand the potential for creative solutions. Emphasizing inclusivity creates a welcoming environment where everyone feels valued and respected.

By developing a system for sharing workloads and lifeloads while gaining guidance within your network, you create a supportive ecosystem that promotes growth, productivity, and fulfillment for all members involved. Through effective communication, boundary setting, collaboration based on strengths, mentorship, mutual support in personal matters, diversity, and inclusion, you cultivate a thriving network that propels everyone toward success in both their professional life and personal life.

As I wrap up this exploration of achieving more by doing less, I hope it's clear that the cultivation of a supportive professional network is pivotal. This network isn't just about accumulating contacts but about building meaningful relationships that can guide, support, and uplift your professional life and your personal life. Through effective collaboration and delegation, you can harness the collective strength of these connections, sharing the burdens and triumphs of your workloads and lifeloads.

Effective collaboration goes beyond mere cooperation; it involves tapping into the diverse strengths and skills of your network to achieve common goals. By delegating tasks strategically, you not only optimize your productivity but also empower others, fostering a sense of trust and mutual respect. This approach not only lightens your load but enriches your professional interactions, leading to more fulfilled and balanced lives.

Moreover, developing a system for sharing workloads is crucial. It ensures that everyone in the network can contribute effectively without facing burnout. This system isn't just about task management; it's about creating an ecosystem where support and guidance flow seamlessly, enhancing the overall productivity and satisfaction of each member.

Throughout this book, I have tackled the toxic culture of busyness that pervades many aspects of modern life. I established that being perpetually busy does not equate to being productive or fulfilled. Instead, adopting a mindful and strategic approach to work and life can lead to significant improvements in both productivity and personal satisfaction. The strategies discussed, including the powerful five-step reTHINK method and the comprehensive wellness plan, are designed to equip you with the tools you need to escape the relentless cycle of busyness.

By rethinking your approach to work and life, engaging deeply with a supportive network, and embracing effective delegation and collaboration, you set the stage for a more productive and fulfilling experience. Remember, true success comes not from how much you do but from how well you do it and with whom you share the journey.

You can then move forward with confidence, knowing that by doing less, you are poised to achieve so much more. You can let go of the practice that more hours equal more productivity and rewire your brain to understand how strategic idleness can actually boost performance. I discussed the importance of setting boundaries and saying no – a powerful tool for preserving mental energy and promoting sustainability in both personal and professional realms.

Cultivating Your Circle: The Strength in Supportive Networks

> **Tip:** For those ready to put these insights into action, start small. Choose one strategy from the book each week and observe how it affects your efficiency and well-being. Engage with colleagues or peers who might also benefit from these approaches, perhaps initiating a discussion group or a workshop based on the methods discussed here.

Although this book provides comprehensive guidance on escaping the busyness trap, I acknowledge that every individual's situation is unique and might require specific adaptations. Continuous learning and adaptation are key; consider further research or exploration in areas particularly relevant to your personal context or industry.

I encourage you to take action today. Do not wait for "the right time," because it might never come; instead, seize the moment now to start making significant changes that lead to a more balanced and rewarding life.

The Broader Context: Embracing a Life Beyond Busyness

At this point you've journeyed through various aspects of overcoming the busyness culture – from creating actionable life plans to developing comprehensive wellness strategies encompassing mental, physical, spiritual, financial, and community well-being. Each chapter has provided tools and insights aimed at helping you adopt a more balanced and fulfilling approach to life.

My five-step reTHINK method has been central to this transformation. I'm going to flip it another way juuuuuuuuust in case you need to read it another way. I really want this to stick because I want YOU to live the life you love, have the career or business you love, and be healthy AF while doing it. Sound good? Good! Let's recap.

Reassess Your Priorities

Take a moment to reflect on what truly matters in your life and career. For instance, if family time is a top priority, consider what it would look like to cut back on late-night work sessions. Delegate tasks at work that others can handle, enabling you to focus on high-impact activities. One of my business besties, Sarah, realized she was spending too much time on administrative tasks. By hiring a virtual assistant, she freed up her schedule to spend more evenings with her kids.

Restructure Your Time

Creating a realistic schedule is key to maintaining productivity without feeling overwhelmed. For example, use a time-blocking method to allocate specific hours for deep work, meetings, and personal time. My friend John found that by dedicating his mornings to focused work and afternoons to meetings and emails, he was able to accomplish more without burning out. Remember to include breaks and leisure activities in your schedule to recharge.

Reallocate Resources

Use your resources – time, energy, and money – wisely. Invest in tools and services that can streamline your workload. For example, using project management software like Notion or Asana can help you keep track of tasks and deadlines efficiently. Consider energy management, too; if you're more productive in the morning, schedule your most challenging tasks then. One of my other business besties, Lisa, invested in a meal delivery service, which saved her hours each week that she could then dedicate to her passion projects.

Cultivating Your Circle: The Strength in Supportive Networks

Rebuild Supportive Networks

Cultivate relationships that offer emotional and practical support. Engage with mentors and peers who can provide valuable feedback. For instance, join professional groups or online communities related to your field. My friend Alex joined a local entrepreneur group where he found not only business advice but also lifelong friends who understand his challenges. Building a support network can provide you with different perspectives and encouragement when you need it most.

Rejuvenate Through Holistic Wellness Practices

Incorporate physical activity, mindfulness, and relaxation into your routine to maintain a healthy balance. For example, start your day with a short yoga session or a brisk walk to energize yourself. One of my dear mentors, Emma, practices mindfulness meditation during her lunch breaks, which helps her stay focused and calm throughout the day. Regularly engaging in activities that nourish your body and mind can significantly enhance your overall well-being.

By implementing these steps, you can achieve greater productivity without falling into the traps of constant overwork and underappreciation. Remember, a balanced life is not only more fulfilling but also more sustainable in the long run.

CHAPTER 12

DIGITAL DISCIPLINE:
HARNESSING TECHNOLOGY FOR TRUE PRODUCTIVITY

"To err is human, but to really foul things up you need a computer."

PAUL R. EHRLICH

In the dim light of early morning, I sat at my desk in my home office, my laptop open before me, its screen flickering softly. Outside, the neighborhood was just beginning to stir, a symphony of distant car horns and the faint murmur of early risers. Inside, the aroma of freshly brewed coffee filled the air, mingling with the scent of rain tapping against the windowpane. As a leadership consultant, my work thrives on technology and demands constant connectivity. Yet lately, I found myself questioning if this ever-present digital companionship was aiding my productivity or anchoring it.

I recalled a client meeting from the previous week when technology had both streamlined our processes and created unforeseen distractions. The tools designed to enhance efficiency had also fostered an environment where immediate responses were expected regardless of the hour. My thoughts were interrupted by a ping from my laptop – a new email arriving in my already overflowing inbox. I sighed deeply, feeling the weight of every unread message like stones in my stomach. It is too darn early in the morning for this. It was this relentless influx of information that often left me feeling more drained than empowered.

As I sipped my coffee, my mind wandered to a recent workshop I had attended about setting boundaries with technology for better work-life balance. The speaker had emphasized how crucial it was to not let technology use spill over into personal time. I remembered nodding along with the crowd but realized now how little I had applied these lessons to my own life. I looked around my house; stacks of papers flanked my laptop while multiple devices lit up with notifications. It struck me then – I needed a real strategy for using technology as an aid rather than letting it dominate my life.

I decided then to make a change. I would start by designating tech-free hours during my day to disconnect entirely and reconnect

Digital Discipline: Harnessing Technology for True Productivity

with other aspects of life that brought joy and relaxation – perhaps reading that novel sitting untouched on my shelf or taking long walks without checking emails every five minutes. As I planned these changes, I felt a mix of apprehension and excitement at reclaiming control over how I engaged with technology. Would setting these boundaries restore balance to my life or simply reveal how dependent I had become on digital connectivity?

Unleashing Your Productivity: Mastering Technology, Not Being Mastered by It

In today's digital age, the line between harnessing technology for productivity and being overwhelmed by it is perilously thin. The promise of technology as a tool for enhancing efficiency is undeniable, yet its pervasive presence can often lead to a counterproductive reliance that dilutes our focus and saps our time. This delicate balance calls for a disciplined approach to digital tools, turning potential distractions into catalysts of productivity.

Balancing Technology with Your Well-Being a la Sex and the City

I was watching another one of my favorite shows, *Sex and the City*, recently and realized that something I saw had been on my mind lately – the connection to technology use and my health (and well-being). The intersection of technology and well-being is crucial yet often overlooked. Continuous connectivity can lead to burnout, stress, and a blurring of lines between work and personal life. Setting boundaries with technology is essential not just for maintaining productivity but also for preserving mental health and fostering a sustainable work-life balance. This section provides actionable advice on how to achieve this balance, emphasizing the importance of disconnection in an always-connected world.

A Quick Primer on *Sex and the City*

Sex and the City is a popular HBO series that aired from 1998 to 2004, following the lives of four women navigating love, careers, and friendship in New York City. The show's protagonist is Carrie Bradshaw, played by Sarah Jessica Parker, a witty and fashion-forward writer who pens a column called "Sex and the City" for a fictional newspaper. Carrie's experiences and those of her friends often form the basis of her column, as she explores relationships and sexuality in the bustling metropolis. Joining Carrie are her three best friends, each with distinct personalities that complement and contrast with one another:

- Samantha Jones (Kim Cattrall): A confident and sexually liberated public relations executive known for her unapologetic approach to life and love
- Charlotte York (Kristin Davis): An art dealer with a more traditional and romantic view of relationships, often seeking her fairy-tale ending
- Miranda Hobbes (Cynthia Nixon): A career-driven lawyer with a cynical outlook on men and relationships

The series follows these four women as they support each other through various romantic entanglements, career challenges, and personal growth.

Okay, so I was watching this episode of *Sex and the City* in which Carrie is struggling with her laptop and declares, "I'm having a long-distance relationship with my computer." Sound familiar? Just like Carrie's love-hate relationship with her trusty Mac, we're all trying to find that sweet spot between staying connected and not

Digital Discipline: Harnessing Technology for True Productivity

losing our minds. Remember when Carrie freaked out because her computer crashed and she lost all her work? That's the kind of tech stress we're trying to avoid here! Now, I'm not saying we need to go full Carrie Bradshaw and use our ovens for shoe storage instead of embracing technology. But maybe we can take a page from her book and learn to set some boundaries.

She was notorious for turning off her phone to focus on writing her column; that's the kind of mindful tech use we're aiming for! Think about it: how many times have you found yourself scrolling through Instagram when you should be working on that big project? Me? My distraction is getting lost in online shoe shopping when I have a deadline looming. We've all been there, right? But here's the thing: just like Carrie eventually learned to balance her love for fashion with her writing career, we can learn to use technology in a way that supports our goals without taking over our lives. It's about creating systems that work for us, not against us.

I remember watching an episode in which Carrie finally embraced email and it changed her life. And, no, I am not talking about early days AOL dial-up. I mean understanding how a tool can make life easier. That's what we're going for here – using tech to enhance our productivity, not hinder it. But we also need to know when to step away, like when Carrie would meet the girls for cosmos and leave her phone at home. Our Golden Girls would NEVER think to use anything that would distract them, and years later, Carrie and her girls didn't either.

So, let's channel our inner Carrie Bradshaw and start thinking about how we can make technology work for us. Maybe it's setting specific times to check emails (like Carrie's dedicated writing hours), or using productivity apps to stay organized (imagine if Carrie had Trello to keep track of her shoe collection!). The key is to recognize when technology is helping us strut confidently through life like

Carrie in her Manolos, and when it's tripping us up like she did in that infamous runway show. By being mindful of how we use our digital tools, we can create a lifestyle that's as fabulous and balanced as a perfectly crafted *Sex and the City* episode. So, what do you say?

Imagine your smartphone as a Swiss Army knife for your daily life. Sounds great, right? But here's the catch: if you don't know how to use each tool properly, you might end up with more cuts than completed tasks. That's exactly what we're diving into here: mastering the art of tech-powered productivity without letting it take over your life. Think about it: how many times have you fallen into the trap of feeling busy but not actually getting anything meaningful done? We've all been there, drowning in a sea of notifications, emails, and half-finished to-do lists. It's like trying to drink from a fire hose of information!

Here's the exciting part: you have the power to flip the script. By understanding the Jekyll-and-Hyde nature of our digital tools, you can transform them from productivity vampires into your personal productivity superheroes. It's not about working harder; it's about working smarter and aligning your tech use with what truly matters to you.

Are you ready to take control of your tech life and start living it up, Carrie Bradshaw style? Let's do this! Let's embark on this journey together, exploring how to create a digital environment that doesn't just keep you busy, but genuinely propels you toward your goals. We'll uncover the secrets to making technology work for you, not the other way around.

Understanding the Double-Edged Sword of Technology

I'm not going to lie to you, friend: technology is a blessing and a curse. We have tools at our fingertips that can streamline our work processes and enhance our productivity, yet the same tools can become distractions that lead to inefficiency and burnout. Overuse can lead to information overload, fragmented attention, and perpetual busyness without real productivity. Overreliance on digital tools can create a false sense of accomplishment while eroding our ability to focus deeply on meaningful tasks. This paradox underscores the central theme of this chapter: technology should be harnessed as a tool to enhance productivity, not as a crutch that fosters dependency.

Prioritizing Your Tools

Start by identifying which tools genuinely aid your productivity versus those that simply fill time. For instance, project management software like ClickUp or Asana can help organize tasks and deadlines efficiently. However, constantly checking social media or nonessential emails can disrupt your workflow and diminish your overall productivity. Implementing structured use of these tools – such as setting specific times for checking emails – can dramatically improve efficiency.

Setting Boundaries with Technology

Setting boundaries is crucial for maintaining a healthy balance between work and well-being. This involves not just physical boundaries, like designated tech-free zones in your home or office, but also temporal ones – establishing clear start and end times for your workday helps prevent burnout. Creating "digital detox" periods, when you step away from screens entirely, can rejuvenate your mental clarity and focus.

Setting boundaries for technology use is not about restricting yourself; it's about creating freedom – freedom from distractions, freedom to focus, and ultimately, freedom to achieve more by doing less. What I appreciate are practical strategies for employing technology in ways that enhance rather than inhibit productivity. From selecting the right tools to optimizing their settings, the focus is on creating a framework that supports your work without dominating it.

Many successful entrepreneurs attribute their productivity to disciplined tech use. Tim Ferriss, US entrepreneur, investor, author, podcaster, and lifestyle guru, famously limits his email checks to twice a day to avoid constant interruptions. Similarly, Arianna Huffington, founder and CEO of Thrive Global, founder of *The Huffington Post*, and the author of 15 books, advocates for unplugging from technology at least an hour before bed to ensure restful sleep – a practice backed by research[1] showing that screen exposure before sleep can interfere with rest quality. Mama Dawn just stares me down until I put my gadgets away. Seems to me like that's the most effective way to get me to chill.

> **Tip:** Setting expectations with colleagues about availability during nonwork hours can help you alleviate the pressure to constantly be online and responsive.

Practical Steps Toward Digital Discipline

The balance between leveraging technology for productivity and maintaining well-being is delicate but essential. Disciplined use of digital tools ensures they serve as aids rather than hindrances in your daily tasks. This balance enhances not only professional efficiency but also personal satisfaction and mental health.

Here are some practical steps to help you harness technology effectively:

- **Audit your tech use:** Identify which apps or devices are indispensable versus those that contribute little to your goals or well-being.

---

[1] Hale, L., & Guan, S. (2015). Screen time and sleep among school-aged children and adolescents: A systematic literature review. *Sleep Medicine Reviews, 21*, 50–58.

- **Establish clear rules:** Set specific times for checking emails or social media to avoid constant disruptions.

- **Create tech-free zones/times:** Designate areas in your home or office where tech use is off-limits.

- **Use productivity apps wisely:** Try tools like RescueTime to track your digital habits and identify areas for improvement.

By applying these strategies, you can transform technology from a source of distraction into an ally in achieving true productivity without compromising your well-being. Through mindful engagement with technology, you can significantly enhance both efficiency and effectiveness in your daily tasks while maintaining a balanced life – a core principle in achieving more by doing less.

A Mindful Approach to Setting Boundaries

Let's talk about how we can make technology work for us, not against us. It's all about being mindful and setting some smart boundaries. Trust me, this can make a world of difference in how productive and balanced you feel.

Establish Designated Times for Use

First things first, let's talk about setting specific times to check our emails and messages. Constant notifications can really mess with our focus. Instead of getting distracted every few minutes, try batching your email and message checks at certain times during the day. This way, you can stay in the zone and get more done without those pesky interruptions.

Use Tools Effectively

Next up, let's make the most of those productivity apps and tools. Whether it's project management software, calendar apps, or note-taking tools, picking the right ones can really streamline our tasks. It's like having a personal assistant! Spend a little time learning how to use these tools to their full potential, and you'll save yourself a lot of hassle. And don't forget, automating repetitive tasks can be a huge time-saver, too.

Maintain a Clutter-Free Digital Workspace

Just like a tidy desk helps us think clearly, a well-organized digital space can do wonders for our focus. Take some time to delete unnecessary files, organize your folders, and make good use of search functions. A structured filing system means you can find what you need quickly, without wasting time digging through a digital mess.

Regularly Audit Your Use

Finally, it's important to regularly check in on how we're using technology. Reflect on which tools are actually helping and which might be more of a distraction. Sometimes, adjusting settings or trying out new apps can unlock even more benefits. And if you find a tool that's not pulling its weight, it might be time to let it go.

By setting boundaries, keeping our digital spaces tidy, and regularly reviewing our tech habits, we can create a productive work environment that supports us rather than hinders us. Plus, using technology strategically helps us maintain a healthier balance between work and personal life. So, let's harness the power of tech and make it work for us!

Run Your Tech, Don't Let Your Tech Run You

Did I run you off? No? Good!

Take a moment to reflect on your relationship with technology and decide whether you might have to take a break, you know ... see

217

other people. It's not just about disconnecting; it's about connecting with purpose and intention. In this fast-paced digital age, you might often find yourself swept away by constant notifications, social media feeds, and endless emails. But what if you chose to navigate this world mindfully?

Setting boundaries for tech use isn't about shutting yourself off; it's about reclaiming your time and energy. Imagine waking up each day with the intention to be present – not just swiping mindlessly through screens but engaging deeply with what truly matters. By integrating mindful practices into your routines, you can reestablish control over our lives. This brings not only productivity gains but also heartfelt connections with loved ones and greater joy in your daily activities.

Technology should serve as a supportive tool, not rule you like a master. When you use it thoughtfully, you can achieve so much more by doing less. It has the power to enhance your efficiency while protecting your well-being and happiness. Each practice you adopt transforms your interaction with your digital spaces into something meaningful – a purpose-driven culture that fosters creativity and collaboration among individuals and teams alike.

So let's embrace this disciplined approach together. Let's step into tomorrow with confidence and clarity, knowing we have harnessed technology to uplift our lives, not overwhelm them. Together, we can create a world where our digital tools empower us to thrive both personally and professionally.

EMBRACING SIMPLICITY

THE PATH TO ENLIGHTENED LEADERSHIP AND A FULFILLING LIFE

"People waste their time pondering whether a glass is half empty or half full. Me, I just drink whatever's in the glass."

— Sophia Petrillo

As we conclude our journey together, let's reflect on the transformative concepts we've explored about breaking free from the relentless grip of busyness and embracing a simpler, more intentional approach to leadership and life. The principles outlined in this book are not just theories but practical, actionable strategies designed to help you, the busy professional or leader, reclaim your time, enhance your productivity, and ultimately lead a more fulfilling life.

Throughout this exploration, I've challenged conventional notions of success and productivity, advocating for a paradigm shift that values quality over quantity, mindfulness over mindless activity, and strategic pauses over constant motion. This epilogue serves as both a recap of the key insights and a call to action, urging you to implement these life-changing practices in your personal and professional spheres.

The Power of Simplicity in Leadership and Life

"Simplicity is the ultimate sophistication."

— Leonardo da Vinci

This profound statement by one of history's greatest minds encapsulates the core philosophy I've been advocating throughout this book. In a world that often equates complexity with competence and busyness with importance, embracing simplicity can be a revolutionary act.

Simplicity in leadership and life doesn't mean oversimplifying complex issues or avoiding challenges. Rather, it's about

- Cutting through the noise to focus on what truly matters
- Making deliberate choices aligned with your values and goals
- Streamlining processes and communication for greater efficiency
- Creating space for creativity, innovation, and deep thinking
- Fostering an environment of clarity and purpose

By adopting a simpler approach, leaders can create more humane, productive, and sustainable practices within their workplaces and beyond. It's about redefining what true success looks like and setting an example that will resonate throughout generations of leaders to come.

Recapping Key Strategies for Simplification

Let's revisit some of the core strategies I've discussed for embracing simplicity in your leadership and life:

- **Prioritize ruthlessly:** Focus on the vital few tasks that drive the most value, both in your personal life and your organization. Use techniques like the Eisenhower Matrix to distinguish between urgent and important tasks.

- **Embrace strategic idleness:** Counterintuitive as it might seem, scheduled downtime can boost creativity and productivity. Make time for reflection, meditation, or simply doing nothing.

- **Practice effective delegation:** Trust your team members with meaningful responsibilities. This not only lightens your load but also fosters growth, engagement, and *trust* among your team.

- **Streamline decision-making:** Develop clear criteria for decisions and stick to them. Avoid decision fatigue by automating or delegating minor choices.

- **Cultivate mindfulness:** Stay present in the moment, whether you're in a meeting, working on a project, or spending time with loved ones. This reduces stress and improves focus.

- **Declutter your physical and digital spaces:** A tidy environment promotes a clear mind. Regularly purge unnecessary items and information.

- **Learn to say no:** Protect your time and energy by declining commitments that don't align with your priorities or values. And remember that you don't need a reason to say no. Your body is telling you exactly what it needs from you.

- **Implement the five-step reTHINK method:** This comprehensive approach helps you reassess your goals, strategies, and actions to ensure they're aligned with your core purpose.

The reTHINK Method: A Blueprint for Simplification

Let's spin the block quickly back to the reTHINK method, a powerful tool for simplifying your approach to leadership and life:

- **R – Reflect:** Take time to pause and consider your current situation, goals, and challenges. Ask yourself probing questions about what's working, what isn't, and why.

- **E – Evaluate:** Objectively assess your priorities, commitments, and use of resources (time, energy, money). Identify areas of misalignment or inefficiency.

- **T – Trim:** Cut away the nonessential. This could mean eliminating unnecessary meetings, streamlining processes, or letting go of projects that no longer serve your core objectives.

- **H – Harmonize:** Ensure that your actions, goals, and values are in alignment. Look for ways to create synergy with the different areas of your life and work.

- **I – Innovate:** Seek creative solutions to simplify complex problems. Challenge assumptions and be open to new approaches.

- **N – Nurture:** Foster an environment that supports simplicity and mindfulness. This includes nurturing relationships, personal growth, and a culture of continuous improvement.

- **K – Kindle:** Keep the flame of simplicity alive by regularly revisiting and reinforcing these principles. Share your insights with others and lead by example.

By consistently applying the reTHINK method, you can create a virtuous cycle of simplification and improvement in all areas of your life and leadership.

The Historical Context of Simplicity

The concept of embracing simplicity is not new, especially in African spiritual and leadership traditions. Throughout history, African leaders and spiritual guides have advocated for a simpler approach to life and governance. One fascinating historical example comes from the Yoruba people of West Africa, in the form of Iyami Aje, often referred to as the "Mothers of Wisdom" or "Spiritual Mothers."

The Iyami Aje are powerful female figures in Yoruba spirituality, believed to possess profound mystical knowledge and the ability to shape destinies. Their teachings emphasize the importance of balance, harmony, and simplicity in both spiritual and worldly affairs. The concept of "Iwa Pele" (gentle character) is central to their philosophy, encouraging leaders and individuals to cultivate humility, patience, and simplicity in their interactions and decision-making processes.

Although the specifics of Iyami Aje teachings might not all be directly applicable to modern leadership, the core principle of embracing simplicity as a path to wisdom and effectiveness remains relevant. This historical perspective reminds us that the struggle against unnecessary complexity is a timeless human challenge, one that has been addressed by African spiritual leaders for centuries.

The Yoruba tradition of Ifa divination, closely associated with the Iyami Aje, further emphasizes the importance of simplicity and clarity in seeking guidance and making decisions. The intricate system of Ifa, although complex in its totality, aims to distill wisdom into simple, actionable insights for leaders and individuals alike.

This focus on simplicity in African leadership extends beyond the spiritual realm. Many traditional African leaders have historically emphasized humility and simplicity as means to foster closer connections with their people and maintain harmony within their communities. This approach stands in contrast to more complex, hierarchical leadership styles often seen in other parts of the world.

By looking to these historical African examples, modern leaders can gain valuable insights into the timeless power of simplicity in effective leadership and decision-making.

Simplicity in the Digital Age

In our modern, technology-driven world, the need for simplicity is perhaps more pressing than ever. The constant barrage of information, notifications, and digital distractions can overwhelm even the most organized leader. Here are some strategies for maintaining simplicity in the digital age:

- **Digital minimalism:** Regularly audit your digital tools and subscriptions. Keep only what truly adds value to your work and life.

- **Batch processing:** Set specific times for checking emails and messages rather than constantly responding to notifications.

- **Mindful tech use:** Be intentional about when and how you use technology. Consider implementing "tech-free" times or zones in your day.

- **Simplify communication:** Use clear, concise language in your digital communications. Avoid unnecessary CCs and lengthy email chains.

- **Leverage automation:** Use technology to simplify repetitive tasks, freeing up your mental energy for more important work.

By applying these principles, you can harness the power of technology while avoiding its potential to complicate and distract.

The Role of Simplicity in Diversity, Equity, and Inclusion

An often-overlooked benefit of embracing simplicity in leadership so that you can achieve more is its positive impact on diversity, equity, and inclusion (DEI) efforts. By simplifying processes, communication, and decision-making, leaders can create a more accessible and equitable environment for all team members. Here's how:

- **Clear communication:** Simple, straightforward communication reduces the potential for misunderstanding and ensures that everyone, regardless of background, can fully participate.

226
Epilogue

- **Transparent processes:** Simplified, well-documented processes make it easier for all team members to understand and engage with organizational systems.

- **Reduced bias:** Simple decision-making criteria can help minimize the impact of unconscious biases.

- **Inclusive culture:** A culture that values simplicity often naturally becomes more inclusive because it reduces unnecessary barriers to entry and participation.

By embracing simplicity, leaders can create an environment where diversity is celebrated, equity is promoted, and inclusion is the norm.

Overcoming Barriers to Simplicity

Although the benefits of embracing simplicity are clear, implementing this approach is not always easy. Leaders often face several barriers when trying to simplify their work and life:

- **Cultural resistance:** In many organizations, busyness is equated with importance. Changing this mindset requires consistent effort and leading by example.

- **Fear of inadequacy:** Some leaders worry that simplifying their approach might make them appear less competent or hardworking.

- **Complexity addiction:** After years of operating in a complex environment, some leaders find it challenging to let go of familiar, albeit complicated, ways of working.

- **Short-term thinking:** The process of simplification often requires an initial investment of time and effort, which can be daunting for those focused on immediate results.

Epilogue: Embracing Simplicity

To overcome these barriers, do the following:

- Communicate the benefits of simplicity clearly and consistently.
- Start small and showcase early wins.
- Provide support and resources for team members as they adapt to new, simpler ways of working.
- Celebrate examples of effective simplification within your organization.

Remember, embracing simplicity is a journey, not a destination. Be patient with yourself and your team as you work toward a simpler, more effective approach.

The Ripple Effect of Simplicity

When you embrace simplicity, the positive effects extend far beyond your own productivity and well-being. A commitment to simplicity can create a ripple effect starting with you personally and reverberating throughout an organization and even into the broader community:

- **Improved team performance:** When you model simplicity, your team members often follow suit, leading to more efficient and effective work across the organization.
- **Enhanced work-life balance:** A simpler approach to work often allows for better boundaries between your professional life and personal life, benefiting employees' overall well-being.
- **Increased innovation:** By clearing away unnecessary complexity, you can create space for creativity and innovative thinking to flourish.

- **Better customer experiences:** Simplified internal processes often translate to smoother, more straightforward experiences for customers and clients.

- **Environmental benefits:** A focus on simplicity can lead to reduced waste and more sustainable practices, benefiting the broader environment.

- **Community impact:** As a leader, when you embrace simplicity in your professional lives, you often carry this mindset into your community involvement, contributing to more focused and effective social initiatives.

By committing to simplicity, you can create positive change that extends far beyond their immediate sphere of influence.

Simplicity and Sustainability

In our era of increasing environmental awareness, it's worth noting the strong connection between simplicity and sustainability. A simpler approach to leadership and life often naturally aligns with more sustainable practices:

- **Resource efficiency:** Simplifying processes often leads to more efficient use of resources, reducing waste and environmental impact.

- **Long-term thinking:** The practice of simplification will encourage you to think beyond short-term gains, aligning with the long-term perspective needed for true sustainability.

- **Focus on essentials:** By prioritizing what's truly important, you can avoid unnecessary consumption and focus on sustainable value creation.

- **Clear communication:** Simplified communication makes it easier to convey sustainability goals and engage stakeholders in environmental initiatives.

- **Mindful consumption:** A mindset of simplicity often translates to more conscious consumption habits, both personally and organizationally.

By embracing simplicity, you can contribute to a more sustainable future for your organizations and the planet.

The Journey Ahead: Implementing Simplicity in Your Life and Leadership

As we wrap up this delightful journey through the art of simplicity in leadership and life – learning to do less so that we can achieve more – let's remember that this isn't a one-time makeover: it's a lifelong adventure. Here are some final nuggets of wisdom to keep you smiling and inspired

- **Start small:** Dip your toes in by trying out one or two simplification tricks in your daily grind. Once you see the magic, you'll be itching to simplify even more.

- **Be patient:** Rome wasn't built in a day, and neither are new habits or cultural shifts. Give yourself and others a break as you work toward a simpler, happier life.

- **Stay flexible:** Consistency is great, but don't be afraid to switch things up as life throws curveballs your way. Simplicity should make life easier, not box you in.

- **Share your journey:** Spread the love! As you reap the rewards of a simpler life, share your stories with friends, family, and colleagues. Your journey can light the way for others.

- **Continuous learning:** Keep that curiosity alive. There's always a new way to simplify and improve, so stay open to fresh ideas and perspectives.

- **Reflect regularly:** Take a breather now and then to look back on your progress and realign your priorities. Self-awareness is your best friend on this journey.

- **Celebrate successes:** Don't forget to pat yourself on the back! Celebrate the wins, big and small, that come from embracing simplicity.

Simply put: as a leader, focus on taking action rather than over-analyzing situations. By embracing simplicity, you're not just making your own life better; you're creating a space where everyone can shine.

You know, watching *The Golden Girls* has taught me so much about doing less to achieve more. Let me share some of the lessons I've picked up from those amazing ladies. First off, they really embrace simplicity. Seeing how they live together in Miami, it's clear that a simple living arrangement can lead to such rich relationships and experiences. Their shared home is the perfect example of how less can be more when it comes to creating a supportive environment. Their communication is another big one. The way they resolve conflicts and misunderstandings through direct, honest conversations is so refreshing. It's a reminder that straightforward communication can help avoid prolonged drama and get to resolutions quickly. Each of them has their own unique strengths, and they really play to those. Instead of trying to be everything to everyone, they leverage what they're good at, and it works beautifully. It's a great lesson in focusing on what you do best. One of the most important things they show is the value of prioritizing relationships. They invest so much time and energy into their friendships, and it pays off in such fulfilling ways. It's a reminder that sometimes, focusing on people rather than material pursuits or busy schedules can lead to a richer life. Their adaptability is also something I admire. They face new challenges with such flexibility and openness, showing that being willing to change can lead to unexpected opportunities and growth without overcomplicating things. And the humor! Their wit and sarcasm are not just entertaining but also a great coping mechanism. They show how humor can be an efficient way to deal with life's challenges, reducing stress and fostering resilience without needing elaborate solutions. Sophia, in particular, brings so much wisdom through her life experiences. She's a great example of how wisdom can lead to simpler, more effective decision-making and problem-solving. Finally, their mutual support is something I find truly inspiring. They rely on each other for emotional and practical support, creating a network that enables them to achieve more collectively than they could individually. It's a beautiful example of how less external support can be needed when you have a strong internal network.

"If you want to fly, you have to give up the things that weigh you down."

– Alice Walker

To all the high-achieving, overworked, people-pleasing superstars out there: you deserve to achieve more by doing less. Yes, I said it! This isn't just a catchy phrase; it's a call to arms for everyone who has ever felt the weight of the world on their shoulders. It's time to drop the performative hustle and embrace a new way of living – one that prioritizes joy, connection, and authenticity over the endless grind.

The Reality of Busyness

Let's be real: *busy* has become a four-letter word, synonymous with overwhelm and exhaustion. We've been conditioned to believe that our worth is tied to our productivity, that the more we do, the more valuable we are. But here's the truth: busyness is not a badge of honor. It's a trap that keeps us from truly engaging with our lives and the people we care about.

Imagine a world where you can say no without guilt, where your to-do list doesn't dictate your worth, and where you can actually enjoy the things you love. This is not a dream; it's a reality waiting for you to claim it.

Finding Your Tribe

Think of this journey as your own Golden Girls moment—where you find your tribe, support each other, and share laughter and wisdom along the way. Surrounding yourself with people who get it is crucial. You need a crew who lifts you up, challenges you, and reminds you that it's okay to step back and breathe.

When you connect with like-minded individuals, you create a space for vulnerability and growth. You share your struggles and triumphs, and in doing so, you realize you're not alone. This community is your lifeline, your cheer squad, and your safe haven.

Embracing the Power of Rest

Let's talk about rest. It's not just a luxury; it's a necessity. In a world that glorifies hustle, taking a break can feel radical. But rest is where the magic happens. It's in those quiet moments that we recharge, reflect, and reconnect with our true selves.

Incorporate intentional downtime into your routine. Whether it's a short walk, a cozy evening with a book, or a weekend getaway, prioritize activities that nourish your soul. When you allow yourself to rest, you come back stronger, more focused, and ready to tackle whatever comes your way.

Redefining Productivity

Here's the kicker: achieving more by doing less doesn't mean you're slacking off. It means you're being intentional with your time and energy.

- **Prioritize:** Not everything on your to-do list deserves your attention. Identify what truly matters and focus on those tasks.
- **Say no:** Every yes is a no to something else. Choose wisely.
- **Delegate:** You don't have to do it all. Trust your team, your friends, and your family to share the load.
- **Embrace imperfection:** Perfectionism is a productivity killer. Let go of the need to be flawless and embrace the beauty of being human.

Cultivating Joy

In our quest for productivity, we often forget the importance of joy. Make time for what lights you up. Dance like nobody's watching, laugh until your sides hurt, and indulge in your favorite hobbies. Joy is not just a feeling; it's a practice.

When you prioritize joy, you create a life that feels rich and fulfilling. You'll find that your productivity increases when you're genuinely happy.

The Ripple Effect of Change

When you choose to live a life beyond busyness, you're not just transforming your own experience; you're creating a ripple effect that can inspire others. Your friends, family, and colleagues will notice your shift in energy and may be inspired to make changes in their own lives.

Imagine a world where we all prioritize well-being over busyness. Together, we can redefine success and create a culture that values balance, authenticity, and connection.

Embracing Flexibility

Life is unpredictable, and that's okay. Embrace flexibility and be open to new opportunities. When plans change, instead of panicking, adapt and see where the new path takes you. This mindset enables you to navigate life's ups and downs without losing your cool.

Creating a Wellness Plan

To truly thrive while doing less, you need a wellness plan that works for you. This isn't a one-size-fits-all approach. It's about creating a personalized strategy that addresses your unique needs. Consider incorporating the following:

- **Mindfulness practices:** Meditation, journaling, or simply taking a few deep breaths can ground you.
- **Physical activity:** Find movement that you enjoy, whether it's yoga, dancing, or hiking.
- **Nutrition:** Fuel your body with nourishing foods that make you feel good.
- **Social connections:** Make time for the people who lift you up and inspire you.

The Journey Ahead

As we wrap up this chapter, remember that transitioning from a life of busyness to one of intention is a journey. There will be bumps along the way, and that's perfectly normal. What matters is that you keep showing up for yourself and your dreams.

You have the power to redefine what success looks like for you. It's not about doing more; it's about being more – more present, more authentic, and more aligned with your values.

A Call to Action

So, here's your challenge: embrace this new way of living. Prioritize what truly matters. Rest without guilt. Play without restraint. Connect deeply with others. Redefine success on your own terms.

Thank you for being a friend and joining me on this path to redefine what it means to be truly productive and fulfilled. Together, we can create a world where "busy" is no longer a badge of honor, but a four-letter word we've outgrown.

As you turn the last page and step back into the hustle and bustle, carry with you the courage to simplify, the strength to say no when it counts, and the wisdom to focus on what truly matters. Your adventure toward a simpler, more fulfilling life starts now. Thank you for being part of this journey. Here's to your continued success, joy, and positive impact on the world. And remember, in the wise words of Dorothy from *The Golden Girls*, "It's not easy being a mother. If it were easy, fathers would do it." Here's to achieving more by doing less. Here's to a life beyond busyness. Here's to you and the beautiful, balanced life that awaits you. Let's step into this journey together and remember you're not just allowed to thrive – you're meant to. So, embrace simplicity and watch as it transforms your leadership and your life. Thank you for being a friend!

The Process Model for Prioritization and Focus (PMPF)

The **Process Model for Prioritization and Focus (PMPF)** is a structured approach designed to help individuals shift from mere activity to meaningful achievement by guiding them through a series of strategic steps. This model consists of four distinct phases, each playing a crucial role in aiding individuals to streamline their efforts toward their core goals and aspirations.

Identify Your Core Goals

The initial phase of the PMPF involves deep introspection to identify and define one's core personal and professional goals. By understanding what success really means on a personal level, individuals can prioritize tasks that directly contribute to these overarching objectives. This phase serves as the foundation for all subsequent actions within the model, ensuring that every effort aligns with these central aspirations.

Evaluate Your Activities

Following the identification of core goals, the PMPF prompts individuals to evaluate their current daily activities against these established objectives. This critical assessment highlights any disparities or areas where activities might not be in alignment with core goals. By scrutinizing each task through the lens of their overarching aspirations, individuals can pinpoint areas for improvement and realignment.

Strategically Eliminate Tasks

In the third phase, the PMPF advocates for strategic elimination of nonessential tasks. By applying criteria such as impact, alignment with core goals, and personal satisfaction, individuals can systematically weed out low-value activities that do not contribute significantly to their overall success. This process allows for a focused approach by freeing up time and energy for endeavors that hold greater importance.

Reallocate and Focus Your Effort

The final phase of the PMPF involves intentional reallocation of resources and energy toward tasks that are in alignment with core goals. By redirecting freed-up time and energy toward meaningful pursuits, individuals can ensure that their efforts are concentrated on activities that contribute most significantly to their desired outcomes. This deliberate reallocation reinforces the importance of sustained focus on meaningful accomplishments over mere busyness.

Conclusion

The PMPF not only provides a structured framework for achieving greater productivity but also instills a practice of regular self-reflection and alignment checks. By following this model, individuals can navigate the complexities of prioritization with clarity and purpose, ultimately leading to a more intentional and fulfilling life.

Understanding the distinction between mere activity and true achievement is more than just a productivity tip; it is a fundamental shift in how you approach your daily life. By prioritizing meaningful achievements, we combat the pervasive culture of busyness that can lead to burnout and dissatisfaction. This appendix has equipped you with the knowledge to identify and eliminate unnecessary activities, enabling you to focus on what truly matters.

Trimming the excess from your schedule is not just about saying no, but about saying yes to a more fulfilling life. The guilt often associated with declining tasks can be overwhelming, yet managing this guilt is crucial for maintaining mental well-being and ensuring your efforts are aligned with your values. By streamlining commitments, you free up resources – time, energy, and attention – to invest in pursuits that are genuinely rewarding.

The practice of evaluating and streamlining efforts is not a one-time task but an ongoing process that requires regular reflection and adjustment. It is about continuously asking yourself whether your current activities contribute to your long-term goals and, if not, having the courage to make necessary changes. This dynamic approach ensures that you remain adaptable and responsive to life's ever-changing circumstances, enabling you to thrive in both personal and professional realms.

By applying these strategies, you are not only enhancing your productivity but also fostering a lifestyle that values quality over quantity. This shift toward intentional living doesn't just lead to better outcomes in projects or tasks; it enriches your life, making each day more purposeful and each achievement more satisfying.

Embrace these changes boldly, knowing that by doing so, you are paving the way for a richer, more productive life. Let this be your guide to breaking free from the chains of busyness and embracing a future where your activities are in true alignment with your aspirations. Remember, the aim is not just to be busy, but to be impactful – where every effort you make is a step toward a significant achievement.

Acknowledgments

First and foremost, I've got to give thanks to God who protects babies and fools. My, my, my, I've been a fool a time or two or three thousand times. And She ain't failed me yet. To my ancestors who whisper to me to rest so I can keep going and to slow down so I can speed up! I hear you.

To my Queenager, my why, Sanai—my greatest gift. You, my darling, are the reason I push the pedal to the metal, but I want you to know that rest is not a reward; it's your responsibility. Remember that, always. Mommy is already SO darn proud of you.

To my Mommy, Mama Dawn, and Daddy, Bernard—thank you for coming to the United States and creating a space where I could leap and soar. Thank you for helping me raise Sanai when divorce caught me like Mike Tyson biting off Evander Holyfield's ear. Your sacrifices are the foundation of my dreams. "Yes, I have a real job!!!"

To my sibs, Anthony and Cinandra, the coolest humans I know. Anthony, you were my first best friend, my singing partner, and my personal stylist. Cinandra, you were my first baby, and watching you grow has been one of my greatest joys. "Y'all got me feeling like I'm in a '90s sitcom, all love and no drama!"

To Emma's grandchildren—keep thriving, not just surviving. We are the future, and I'm so proud of each of you. "Keep shining like the stars you are, fam!"

To my Sorors of Delta Sigma Theta Sorority, Incorporated, who have helped shape me into who I am today, including Angela, Timyiaka, Dionna, Liz, and my home chapter, Xi Tau Chapter of Delta Sigma Theta Sorority, Inc.—your sisterhood is my strength. To my spec fam and specials, namely: Adia, Bukky, Chantel, Nikki, Sharmayne, and EJ—you all add a special sparkle to my life. Thank you for being MY CREW. "Y'all my day ones, for real!" "My Sorors, y'all got me feeling like Beyoncé at Coachella!"

To my cheerleaders, Brianna and Soror Besties Ajuah and FranCee, and my Sister, Rochelle—thank you for helping me traverse the tricky terrain of being a divorcee, single mom, and entrepreneur. Your support is a gift. "Y'all my ride-or-dies, no cap!"

To J.A.C.K.—Chanel and Julia and Amicizia–Mallory, Becky, and Dana. You threw me a lifeline when I was drowning. I am forever grateful. "Y'all came through like a Hail Mary in the fourth quarter!"

To Maria and Naimah—you remind me of my power daily. Thank you for being my mirrors and my motivators. "Y'all keep me grounded and glowing!"

To my team—Blythe and Alicia. You say yes to every harebrained scheme, every time I forgot my slides until the day before I needed them, when I booked myself to the wrong city, and through the lean times. I COULD NOT run this race without you two.

To Kaine, the best Godfather in the world—your love and support mean everything. You stood in the gap for years and I cannot thank you enough. "You the real OG, Kaine!"

To my therapists throughout the decades—thank you for walking alongside me as I figured ME out. Your guidance has been invaluable. "Y'all my mental health MVPs!"

To my amore, Allan—thank you for giving me cover to learn to love again, starting with really loving myself. You're the perfect plan I never thought of. "That's a good man, Savannah." Tee-hee.

And finally, to everyone who has been part of this journey—thank you for believing in me, even when I didn't believe in myself. This book is as much yours as it is mine. "Let's keep leveling up and breaking barriers, one four-letter word at a time!"

Index

249

Index

251

Index

252

Index

255